Sept.

Dear Jonathan and Gail —
    Enjoy reading about your
amazing sister!
            Best wishes,
            Debby Flanebaum

The Jewish Woman Next Door

Repairing the World One Step at a Time

THE JEWISH WOMAN NEXT DOOR

REPAIRING THE WORLD
ONE STEP AT
A TIME

DEBBY FLANCBAUM

URIM PUBLICATIONS
Jerusalem • New York

The Jewish Woman Next Door: Repairing the World One Step at a Time
by Debby Flancbaum

Copyright © 2007 by Debby Flancbaum
Printed at Hemed Press, Israel. First Edition.
ISBN-13: 978-965-7108-95-6
ISBN-10: 965-7108-95-0
Urim Publications
P.O. Box 52287, Jerusalem 91521 Israel

Lambda Publishers Inc.
3709 13th Avenue Brooklyn, New York 11218 U.S.A.
Tel: 718-972-5449 Fax: 718-972-6307, mh@ejudaica.com

www.UrimPublications.com

To

Lou

Rachel, Jessica

Aleeza

and

Dad and Mom.

I love you all like crazy!

I always have…and I always will.

CONTENTS

Foreword

by Louis Flancbaum, MD

Israel's deliverance [from Egypt] was in reward for the righteous women.
Talmud, Sotah 11b

Jews are fortunate to live in the United States. In the 21st century, we enjoy a level of acceptance, influence and prosperity in America never before realized. We're also lucky to be here at this time in history because the American ideal of a "melting pot," where everyone blended together and gave up their unique cultural and ethnic traits, has gradually given way to the recognition of the value of a societal "mosaic" or "salad," in which people are encouraged to maintain their own identities. Jews have fully integrated into virtually all spheres of American life, from the board room to the Congress, while still being able to be themselves.

At the same time, girls growing up in this culture are constantly bombarded by mixed-messages from television, radio, movies, and music. You are all aware of the negative stereotypes about African-Americans, Hispanic-Americans, and Asian-Americans. But, are you also aware of the negative stereotypes about Jews, especially Jewish women? These derogatory caricatures not only affect how others think about us or we them, but also how we think about ourselves. They can lower our confidence and self-esteem and deter us from trying to be as successful as possible.

As is true of most stereotypes, the ones about Jewish women are false. Throughout Jewish history, women have played critical roles in guaranteeing the survival of the Jewish people. In the Torah, women acted primarily to secure the spiritual future of the Jewish people. Sarah persuaded Abraham to send Haggar and Ishmael away, and Rebecca tricked Isaac into giving Jacob the birthright. The actions of these two matriarchs helped provide stability to the Jewish nation. During the period of slavery in Egypt, women, led by the prophetess Miriam, played pivotal roles in maintaining a "normal" life and preserving the integrity of Jewish family life. When Pharaoh decreed that all Jewish male children be killed, Miriam's father, Amram, suggested that the Jews have no more children. Miriam successfully argued with her father and convinced him that his idea was worse than Pharaoh's, because Pharaoh's decree only affected half of the children, whereas her father's plan affected all of them. Also during the slavery, the women made great efforts to remain attractive to their husbands and maintain a normal, cohesive family-life. Their righteousness was later rewarded by their mirrors being incorporated into the *laver* (washing station) of the *mishkan* (tabernacle). And finally, when the men lost faith in God and built the Golden Calf, the women remained true and did not participate in this sin.

During the times of the prophets, women's roles were expanded to encompass the physical survival of the Jewish people. Hannah prayed so intently to God for children that she was ultimately rewarded with a son, Samuel, who became a prophet and judge, and anointed Saul, Israel's first king. Her actions are considered the model for prayer and are commemorated on the first day of Rosh Hashana, when her story is read as the *Haftorah*. Deborah was a prophetess and judge and successfully led Israel in battle, while Yael aided her by seducing and killing the Cananite general Sisera. Women were also the heroes of the Purim and Chanukah stories. Esther eventually exposed Haman's scheme to murder Jews to King Achasverosh and Judith calmed and baited Holofernes, the enemy general, then beheaded him in his sleep allowing the Macabees to prevail. Finally, throughout Jewish history, women have served as role models because of their acts of *chesed* (loving-kindness) and self-sacrifice in the face of adversity. In another *megillah*, Ruth, a Moabite widow, maintained her allegiance to her widowed mother-in-law, Naomi, by converting to Judaism after the death of her own husband. So great were her acts of kindness and faith, that she was rewarded by becoming the great-grandmother of King David, from whose family Jewish tradition tells us that the Messiah will come.

During the Middle Ages, Spanish Inquisition, and more recently, during the Holocaust, when Jews were victims of the crusades, pogroms, and mass extermination, Jewish women always displayed extraordinary bravery. In the face of such terrible adversity, they tried to protect their children and maintain some semblance of a normal Jewish family life, while keeping faith in God. Hannah Senesh was a young European girl who emigrated to Israel before WWII. During the war she returned to Europe as a member of the Israeli underground in order to try to assist the resistance and help Jews escape to Palestine. She was caught and executed as a spy.

Jewish women also played major roles in the establishment of the modern State of Israel. Golda Meir was instrumental in the founding of the state and eventually became Prime Minister, the highest office in the land. Since then, women have continued to serve proudly in the Israel Defense Forces.

In *The Jewish Woman Next Door*, Deborah Biskin Flancbaum continues this rich tradition by profiling contemporary Jewish women engaged in extraordinary acts of *chesed*. These women come from all walks of life and all branches of Judaism. Some perform these acts part-time and others devote a major portion of their life to these efforts. In some cases they work quietly behind the scenes, while in others, these incredible women risk their lives for other Jews they do not even know. They are the modern day Miriams, Deborahs, Esthers, and Ruths, heroines and role models that I want my two daughters, Shira, Tova, and my granddaughter Aleeza, to admire and emulate. It is about these modern heroines, as well as their historic ancestors, that the sages wrote: "Israel's deliverance was in reward for the righteous women."

Introduction

On television and in movies, Jewish women are often portrayed as neurotic, overbearing and materialistic caricatures. These stereotypes represent a subtle form of anti-Semitism thinly veiled as humor. Jewish girls and women are supposed to laugh at these shrill, vain caricatures that cling relentlessly to their children. If we are not amused, we are accused of being overly sensitive or unable to take a joke. Growing up, these images are incorporated into our collective soul and we begin to see ourselves through a distorted lens. The negative perceptions that others have of us, and the images that some of us have of ourselves, motivated me to prove what I already knew – that Jewish women play varied and significant roles in the lives of their families, friends and communities. I'm sure that if you look around you, at the Jewish women in your circle, you'll find that most debunk all of the popular myths about Jewish women.

I set out to create a book that would faithfully and positively showcase Jewish women as they are, not as they appear in the media. These women come from all walks of life and reside in many parts of America and are different in every conceivable way. They appear in all ages, shapes, sizes and coloring, and identify with every branch of Judaism. Yet they share a commitment that links them together – they all perform acts of loving-kindness. Through the work that they do, they are involved in *tikkun olam* (repair of the world). These women are true Jewish-American princesses.

Judaism elevates daily tasks and makes them holy. Each time we recite a *b'racha* (a blessing) before eating a piece of food, we transform the ordinary function of eating into the extraordinary act of thanking God. Often it is Jewish women who sanctify everyday life by routinely using their gifts to imbue the mundane with the sacred, tuning extraordinary actions into meaningful lives. It is my hope that reading the biographical essays of these women will inspire you to become involved in the repair of the world in which we live. By reading these portraits and the explanations of the various *mitzvot* (commandments), you will understand the profound connection between social activism and Judaism.

All of the women featured in this anthology have varied responsibilities to family and community. Many wash dishes, pay bills and put out the garbage. Others take care of aging parents, change diapers, write college term papers, drive car-pools, help with their children's homework, or deal with teenage rebellions. Most women have the capacity to juggle chores, work, children, husbands and friends, somehow successfully keeping all of the balls in the air, and these women are no different.

Why do these women do what they do? What makes their endeavors uniquely Jewish? Often, even the most secular woman can trace her motivation to perform *mitzvot* to a Jewish value or experience first encountered in childhood. Perhaps it was something she studied in a Hebrew School text or absorbed by sitting at her grandmother's knee, but at some moment, the idea of doing an act of loving-kindness emanated from a Jewish source.

I imagine these stories will remind you of a Jewish woman who has affected your life. Perhaps the unique qualities of that woman have been taken for granted, or perhaps the beautiful and precious attributes of someone so close to home have gone unnoticed. Take some time and look closely at the women in your own family and community in a way you may not have looked at them before. Is there someone who is performing extraordinary deeds of loving-kindness that you haven't appreciated? Is there a woman after whose life you would like to pattern your own? Is there anyone performing *mitzvot* with whom you would like to involve yourself now?

These women you will read about represent a broad spectrum of

Jewish lifestyles, from the most traditional to the most liberal, but certain tenets remain constant for all. Rabbi Simlai taught: "The Torah begins with deeds of loving-kindness and ends with deeds of loving-kindness. It begins with deeds of loving-kindness, as it is written, 'And the Lord made for Adam and for his wife garments of skins and clothed them' (Genesis 3:21). It ends with deeds of loving-kindness, as it is written, 'And he was buried in the valley of the land of Moab'" (Deuteronomy 34:6). So begins and ends the lives of our true Jewish heroines.

Section 1

Pidyon Sh'vuyim / Redeeming Captives

Ransom a captive before you feed the poor. No act of charity is greater; and money collected for any purpose whatsoever may be used as ransom — even if collected to build a synagogue.
R. Joseph Caro, Shulchan Aruch

If you think of Jewish women only as passive observers in dangerous situations and not as active participants — think again! In this section you will meet women who have performed the most extraordinary feats, sometimes heroically risking their own safety to bring other Jews to freedom.

From Biblical times onward, Jewish women have played a central role in freeing other Jews from captivity. At each Passover Seder, we gather around the table and recount the story of the Exodus, in which God, with the help of Moses, Aaron and their sister Miriam, redeemed the people of Israel from slavery in Egypt. The Exodus is a central event in Judaism, and of such monumental significance to the Jewish nation that we recall it daily in our prayers, every week in our *Shabbat* rituals, and on every holiday. Miriam was a key player in our escape. It was Miriam who protected her brother, Moses, from death at Pharoah's hand, thereby allowing him to grow into manhood and become the leader of the Jews. Finally, as Israelites were freed from the Egyptians who drowned in the Red Sea, it was Miriam who led the women in dance and song. The verse they chanted is one of the most famous in the Torah, "Sing to the Lord for He has triumphed gloriously. Horse and driver he has hurled into the sea" (Exodus 15:21).

Jewish women have a long history of social activism on behalf of oppressed Jews fulfilling the *mitzvah* of *Pidyon Sh'vuyim* (redeeming captives). During the past century, Jewish women have had opportunities to redeem other Jews from all corners of the globe. In the aftermath of the Nazi horrors, women like Henrietta Szold and Ruth Gruber worked to resettle survivors in Palestine, Europe, Canada and the United States. Women's organizations such as Hadassah were at the forefront of the youth *aliyah* (settling in the land of Israel) movement, which brought approximately 10,000 children and teenagers, many of whom were without family, from war-torn Europe to Palestine.

In the 1960s, 70s and 80s American Jews became aware of the oppression of Soviet and Syrian Jews, who were being held as political prisoners. Jewish women put a tremendous amount of pressure on our government to help facilitate the release of those who were desirous of political, religious and economic freedom. They staged protests, wrote letters, circulated petitions, and traveled to the Soviet Union to show their solidarity. Women such as Alice Sardell fought for the freedom of Syria's 4,000 Jews who were being held as political hostages. She was their voice when they had none.

Since the 1970s, Jews from Israel and the United States have worked tirelessly to bring thousands of Ethiopian Jews to the Land of Israel in order to escape persecution, poverty and famine. Barbara Ribacove Gordon helped bring the plight of Ethiopian Jews to the international stage. Today, she continues to work toward the goal of rescuing all Ethiopian Jews from bondage and bringing them to safety.

Ruth Gruber

A Safe Haven

"Every life has a defining moment and for me that moment came in the summer of 1944 when I helped to bring nearly 1,000 refugees to safe haven in America," says Ruth Gruber, an award-winning journalist. "That trip changed my life. I knew at that moment that I would spend the rest of my life involved in the rescue of Jews."

"World War II and the Holocaust were still raging in Europe." she explains. "President Franklin Delano Roosevelt announced 'that approximately 1,000 refugees should be immediately brought from Italy to this country.'" They would come in as his guests.

Ruth realized that these refugees were going to be exhausted, disoriented and frightened after all they had lived through. She believed it was imperative that someone be with them on their journey to America to ease their way. She suggested the plan to Harold L. Ickes, Secretary of the Interior, for whom she was working as Special Assistant. Ickes thought it was a wonderful idea and decided to send her. In those days it was highly unusual for a woman to be allowed to engage in such a daring mission. Her participation had to be approved though many channels, but finally she was granted permission.

"The voyage was top secret and dangerous," Ruth says. "For my protection, I was made a 'simulated general.' If the Nazis captured me or shot me down, they might kill me if I were an ordinary soldier, but as a General, they had to give me food, clothing, and shelter and keep me alive."

Traveling aboard the A.T.S. Henry Gibbins, they were part of a huge army convoy of twenty-seven vessels. Nazi bombers and U-boats were ominously close by. At night, they cut through the water like ghosts with no lights on and no people on deck.

"They had come from eighteen countries that Hitler had overrun," says Ruth. "Most were Jews, but many were Protestants, Catholics, and Greek Orthodox. They were all ages, from eighty to an infant born in a Jeep and dubbed 'international Harry.' Among them were: Mathilda, who had run an underground rescue station; Leo, an opera star from Zagreb; Edith, who had fought with the Yugoslav partisans; and Manya, who survived five concentration camps to become the group's first bride."

In Ruth's book, "Haven," which recounts the story of the refugees' journey to freedom, she writes, "These people were a cross-section of European life, people who had survived because they scratched and tore and hid and bought false identity papers, and never believed in their own death. I realized that every one of them was alive by a miracle."

On the ship, Ruth was a confidant and a source of strength for the refugees. They came to call her "Mother Ruth." She shared their joys and sorrows, brought their stories to life, and assured them a place in history with her book 'Haven.'

"I often had to stop writing," Ruth says, "because tears were wiping out the words in my notebook. I hoped, through their stories, America might learn the truth of Hitler's crimes."

On August 3, 1944, the ship arrived in New York Harbor. It was the very same day that Anne Frank was captured. Ruth and the refugees were ferried across the water to Hoboken, New Jersey, where she led a press conference introducing some of the refugees and their stories to members of the American press.

They then boarded a train for Oswego, a small town in upper New York state. Some were shocked by their first glimpse of the army camp, Fort Ontario, which was to be their home. It had a chain-link fence topped with barbed wire. One of the refugees turned on Ruth, "How could you bring us to another camp, after the terrible camps we escaped from?" Ruth tried to convince him that all U.S. army camps are surrounded by a fence, but many told Ruth, "Don't let him upset you. We're so happy to be in America. And we feel safer protected by a fence."

"Inside the camp, reporters and photographers swarmed around us," Ruth says, "catching the weary and frightened eyes of the elderly, the tentative smiles of the teenagers, and the lost look of children without shoes. Within a few days, townspeople were hurrying along the other side of the fence bringing gifts to the children. One little girl gave her Shirley Temple doll to one of our children, who had never owned a doll."

For a month, they were placed in quarantine that required that no one could leave the base or receive visitors so that army officers could ask them questions about what they had lived through. Although some had experienced shock and fear on arrival, they quickly relaxed when they realized that the officials were kind and food was plentiful. After a short time, their spirits were high and they were optimistic about their futures.

The rooms in the barracks were the first private space many had had in as long as five years while they were trying to escape Hitler's armies. The hard army cots, the army sheets and blankets, and the table and chair felt like the height of luxury. Some of the women improved upon their surroundings by making curtains and bookshelves and pasting newspaper pictures on the walls.

"The schools of Oswego opened their arms to our children," Ruth reports, "and the children brought America and the Bill of Rights into the camp."

In the weeks and months that followed, the refugees began finding ways to keep themselves occupied. They organized classes in everything from music and literature to woodworking. The people of Oswego formed the "fence society." They visited the refugees, delivered care packages and made conversation. The unofficial anthem became "Don't Fence Me In," a song that was popular during that era.

The winter of 1944 was one of the coldest on record in Oswego. The refugees were confined to a snowy camp, and the mood was somber. The war appeared to be ending, and as a result, they constantly worried about their status. Since they were neither prisoners of war nor illegal immigrants, but guests of the President, they had no status. Moreover, they had signed a paper before boarding the ship, promising that they would return to Europe following the end of the war. "They would have signed anything," says Ruth, "to escape the terror and the bombings." But what would they be returning to?

With help from people like Eleanor Roosevelt, Harold Ickes, and a few others, Ruth continued to fight for them. She even brought a team of Jewish and non-Jewish leaders to ask President Harry Truman to grant them permission to stay here.

"Then on December 23," Ruth says, "as a Christmas present, President Truman announced on the radio that the refugees in Oswego could stay. They had to leave the United States on busses, cross the Rainbow Bridge into Canada, shake the hand of the American consul, receive a visa, and re-enter the United States." They eventually became United States citizens.

Ruth Gruber, who is now in her nineties, was subsequently involved in a great many efforts to redeem Jews from captivity. Her book, *Haven*, was made into a four-hour miniseries by CBS and is now available on DVD. Ruth chronicled the activities of the ship, Exodus 1947, which brought Holocaust survivors to the Holy Land, and she was involved in the rescue of thousands of Jews from Yemen, Iraq, Romania, the former Soviet Union, and most recently from Ethiopia.

Barbara Ribacove Gordon

The Revealing Moment

Barbara Ribakove Gordon was in the process of learning as much as she could about Judaism and Jewish history when she was offered an opportunity to visit the concentration camps of Europe. Although that was canceled, a few days later, she was invited on a trip to learn about the conditions facing Romanian Jewry. Barbara said, "I figured that it was more important to spend my time working on behalf of living Jews than to visit dead ones." On her mission to Romania, Barbara was disturbed to find out that many Jews there were denied the right to emigrate. When she came back to the United States, she began advocating for the release of two families and was successful in her efforts. She says, "I knew after my first experience with rescuing Jews that I could actually have an impact."

Thus in 1981 Barbara joined a group of a dozen other brave souls from North America and traveled to Ethiopia to validate the distressing stories that were coming out of that country. Word was just beginning to spread throughout the international Jewish community that Ethiopian Jews were suffering intolerable hardships and persecution. As Jews worldwide were slowly learning about these poor people's plight and mobilizing to rescue them, Barbara and her companions were the first to embark on an historic fact-finding mission.

This weary bunch had to travel through Ethiopia by mule, foot and horseback, through huge rocky mountains with precipitous drops. Terrified of heights and even more afraid of mules, Barbara lacked the appropriate clothing or supplies for the grueling terrain. During the day, the blazing sun beat down on their heads, and at night they froze without sweatshirts or enough blankets. Several became gravely ill with food poisoning. Barbara, a writer for a health magazine, was the closest thing they had to a doctor or nurse. Her new friends depended on her to administer first aid using the tiny kit she had brought along in case someone had a headache or a blister. Never did she envision that she would have to apply antibiotic ointment to her own backside, covered with painful saddle sores.

One night they slept fitfully on the ground, huddled together, as they heard the chilling sounds of leopards howling in the surrounding trees. They did not have the luxury of giving in to terror or apprehension. They had to move forward.

Barbara, a citified mother and freelance writer, was naïve enough to think that this trip would be an adventure, and never anticipated that she would actually be risking her life. After an exhausting two day journey (there was then no direct way to fly to Ethiopia) they arrived only to be denied authorization to go to Jewish villages in Gondar Province, home to many Jews and ordinarily easily accessible.

With the help of the Mossad (Israel's version of the C.I.A.) the Jews were already trickling out of Ethiopia and making their slow aliyah (immigration to Israel) through Sudan. The then-communist Ethiopian government, in an attempt to isolate and punish them, refused to allow them visitors.

However, Barbara and her colleagues did not make this long trip to sit idly by in hotel rooms. They were determined to see first-hand the conditions in which Ethiopian Jews were living, and devised what they thought was a clever strategy to outsmart the local officials. In order to meet Jews in a tiny and remote village in the Semian Mountains, they pretended to go on safari, and it wasn't until the travelers actually began this arduous trek that they began to doubt the sanity of their plot. Perhaps it was they who had been outwitted. When they arrived in the Jewish village of Shewada, tired, hungry and miserable, they found people who were desperately poor and malnourished. The children were covered with flies. Surprisingly, the

Jews at first did not want the visitors. They did not believe that these white people could possibly be Jews; after all, in their experience all Jews were black. They previously had unpleasant encounters with missionaries posing as Jews, who tried to convert them and their children. Even though it was possible that these strangers might offer desperately needed food or supplies, these proud Ethiopians refused to bend their principles by providing access to their impressionable children.

However, Brett Goldberg, a member of the group and a linguist from Yale who spoke Amharic (the Ethiopian language), gradually gained their trust. He persuaded the Ethiopians to permit the travelers to view the village synagogue, which was a round stone hut that looked unlike any other synagogue they had ever seen. The Torah was contained in a book, instead of a scroll, and was written in the Ethiopian religious language, Ge'ez, rather than in traditional Hebrew. These disoriented, sick and weary travelers were afraid to admit, even to themselves, that they might have made a huge mistake in coming to this country. How could they make real contact with these unfamiliar people, living in the middle of nowhere, in horrible conditions, without a "real" Torah or a "real" synagogue. There was suddenly an unspoken undercurrent of doubt as they wondered if they had endured hardship for nothing. Then, for some reason that no one could quite understand, one member of the group asked an Ethiopian Jewish elder, "Which Torah portion are you reading this *Shabbat?*" The Ethiopian leader replied, "We will be chanting *Parshat Noach* (the story of Noah), which was the same section that Jews all over the world were reading that week.

This answer represented a transcendental moment for Barbara and the others. Somehow these people, living in squalor and isolated from the rest of the Jewish world (in fact, from the entire world), without watches, telephones, or any other form of communication, remained in synch with Jews everywhere. Even those among the travelers who were not religiously observant realized the amazing connection that had just been made, surpassing time, space, distance, skin color and culture. Indeed, they were all Jews.

By 1991, Barbara had become the founder and executive director of NACOEJ, the North American Conference on Ethiopian Jewry, and was intimately involved in relief and rescue, including Operation Solomon. Because of the raging civil war, the Jews in Ethiopia were in increasingly more danger. The United States and Israel persuaded the opposing factions to make a temporary cease-fire so that the Jews could safely make their way out. The two armies stood motionless while forty-one El Al flights, packed with Jewish refugees, flew them to the Land of Israel. This twentieth century miracle of Jewish life, a modern day Exodus story, occurred largely because a New York journalist took a leap of faith and traveled on an uncharted path to rescue other Jews from bondage. Today NACOEJ is still providing aid for thousands of Ethiopian Jews who have not yet left for Israel, and in Israel offers essential educational programs for the community.

Alice Sardell

Follow Your Vision

"God presents us with *mitzvot* that can be miracles waiting to happen," says Alice Sardell. "Sometimes they just look like choices to take or not take as we see fit. It is up to us to trust, to have faith in God that it is the right thing, that it has your name on it." Alice, a native New Yorker, a second generation American Syrian Jew, and an attorney in her early thirties, was establishing a career and raising her young daughter Evelyn. Together with other members of her community, Alice helped to found the first Syrian Jewish congregation in Manhattan and got to know the young cantor whom they hired. He was the eldest of ten children and from Damascus. With great difficulty, he had managed to leave Syria on a student visa to attend school at Yeshiva University.

Gradually, Alice's life took on a new direction. On their walks home after services, the cantor told her about the plight of the Jewish community in Syria. There were 4,000 Jews in Syria, in the cities of Damascus, Aleppo, and Kamishli. Although since 1948, the year Israel was created, they were allowed to work and quietly practice their religion, they were not permitted to travel outside of Syria. There were many divided families with the mother and a few children in Syria, and the father and a child in New York. The Jews who managed to leave Syria did so by escaping. While there were some successful escapes, it was extremely dangerous, and if caught the Jews would be killed. The Jews in Syria lived in ghettos and were monitored on a 24 hour-a-day basis by Syria's secret police. Jews who were arrested were subject to torture, tortures that the Syrians learned from Alois Brunner, a nazi who escaped Germany after World War II and lived in Syria, under

Syrian protection. The Jews in Syria lived in fear. "I felt passionate that in 1989 no country should be allowed to deny anybody the basic human right of travel," recalls Alice. "As a mother, I felt even more passionate that families must be reunited. Despite the fact that I had no experience in international relations, I had no doubt that this *mitzvah*, this rescuing of the 4,000 Jews had my name on it. I knew what had to be done and that it would be my faith in God that would guide me and free my people. I also knew that it would require years of hard work. It was during a trip to Israel, standing beside the grave of Golda Meir, the former Prime Minister, pondering the strength and courage of this amazing woman, that I felt the choice had been made and that I would commit myself entirely to rescuing Syria's Jews. Inspired by the memory of Golda Meir, I knew that I had to meet this challenge as a Jewish woman.

Together with other members of the Syrian Jewish community in New York, Alice formed "The Council for the Rescue of Syrian Jews." They set out to educate the United States Government and the world about the plight of Syria's Jews. The United States Department of State was very discouraging and told Alice that the Jews in Syria would never be free until there is peace with Israel. That did not stop her, it only made her more determined. Together with her group they educated congressmen, senators, the State Department, the White House, and it did not stop there. "Every King, every President, every Prime Minister, who was going to Syria, met first with me and my group and were briefed on Syria's 4,000 Jews," explains Alice. "And as a result of what they learned from us, each and every person asked President Assad of Syria, 'What about the Jews?' I knew that the more a light was shone on them, the safer they would be and the quicker they would be free."

She organized rallies in New York, in Washington, in Europe, and Australia. At a rally in London, she released 1,000 balloons that read "Freedom for Syrian Jews." She met with Syrian Government officials, and testified before Congress about the situation of Syria's Jews. Alice was relentless. "I spent my days thinking of what next to do, and who next to call. I spoke on the radio, and on television. I met with European governmental officials and urged them to deny money to Syria until they released the Jews. And they did. And just like water dripping on a rock, the rock began to break. The Syrian Government allowed a young girl, Silva, and her brother, Faraj, to be rejoined with their parents, whom they hadn't seen for eight years. It was a start. Then they allowed a few more people to be reunited with their families here in New York. I knew that while we were making progress, reuniting the divided families was not enough. I wanted everyone out." The Syrian Government then asked Alice to stop the rallies and the legislation in Congress. She explained to them that it was out of her hands. Alice knew that success was in sight and she persevered. Finally in April of 1992, two days after the Passover seder where we retell the story of how God took the Jews out of Egypt, the Syrian Government agreed to allow the Jews in Syria the right to travel. Through the generosity of Mr. Edmond Safra, the Jews of Syria were all provided with airline tickets to exit. It took two more years after that to free all the Jews in Syria. Today most of them live in Brooklyn, New York with their families, in freedom.

In the spring of 1994, at the closing celebration of the Council for the Rescue of Syrian Jews, in New York, three eight-year-old boys from Aleppo who came to sing stood in front of the 300 people assembled. "When I asked them what would they like to sing, they unanimously replied *Hatikvah*." As all present stood with tears in their eyes, listening to the sweet young voices sing about the Israel they had yearned for, I knew that my mission was finally and successfully complete.

Section 2

Tzedakah / Righteousness

Charity equals all other commandments.
Babylonian Talmud, Bava Batra 9a

You or your mother may keep a *tzedakah* box on the kitchen counter. Perhaps it is the blue metal variety, or maybe it is a fancy one that rests on the living room coffee table. Whatever it looks like, its purpose is the same, to be a receptacle for money that Jews collect to help others.

It is commonly believed that the Hebrew word *tzedakah* means charity. Although it is often used that way, literally translated it means "righteousness." Jewish tradition considers it right and proper to give to those in need. In doing so we contribute to the repair of the injustices in the world *(tikkun olam)*. Executing justice through *tzedakah* is considered a *mitzvah*, and therefore, obligatory behavior. "Even a poor man, a subject of charity, should give charity" (BT, Gitten 7b).

The Book of Ruth, which is read on the festival of *Shavuot*, illustrates how two famous Jewish women, Ruth and Naomi, are able to sustain themselves by gleaning the fields. Farmers purposely left a certain portion of their crops for the poor, and at the end of each day Ruth and Naomi collected this food.

Providing for others is such an integral part of Jewish life that Jewish women customarily give charity each Friday night prior to blessing the Sabbath candles by placing some coins in the *tzedakah* box. This small act offers an opportunity to show concern for fellow human beings before offering personal prayers.

Jewish women have traditionally taken this *mitzvah* seriously and have performed it diligently. Some work tirelessly for Jewish organizations such as Hadassah, Amit, Ort, Emunah or Jewish Federations; some volunteer for secular charities. Others, develop imaginative programs to fill existing voids in their communities. As the *Talmud* notes, "Happy are the ones who use their insight when giving to the poor." Each of the women featured in this section derives great joy from the strong sense that she is engaged in something meaningful and right.

Naomi Eisenberger

The Tzedaka Lady of New Jersey

How many people wake up every morning, arrive at their desks by 6:00 a.m., stay there until 9:00 p.m. and talk about how privileged they feel to do what they do? One such individual is Naomi Eisenberger, Managing Director of the Ziv Foundation.

About thirteen years ago, Naomi was serving as president of her synagogue in Millburn, New Jersey. About to go on a vacation to the beach with her husband, Jerry, and her children, Andrew and Sarah, she asked the rabbi for something to read. Naomi wanted something more "substantial" than the mystery novels she had been inhaling. Fortuitously, her rabbi brought her into his study and handed her the book, "Gym Shoes and Irises" by Danny Siegel. The rabbi explained to her that Danny was an icon in the Jewish community – a dynamic speaker, writer and educator involved in some tremendously important *tzedakah* work. Some of Siegel's works focused on his "*mitzvah* heroes" – people who devote themselves to the repair of the world.

Already intrigued, Naomi packed the book along with her sun screen. "I was really blown away by what I read," she recalls. "It was so mind boggling to learn about the creative ways in which people could bring about *tikkun olam*." Danny's work got me thinking about things I could do.

When Naomi got back to New Jersey, she and the rabbi decided to bring Danny to their synagogue as the scholar-in-residence over a *Shabbat*. "Danny helped us establish a *tzedakah* committee called 'Hearts and Hands.' We raised a lot of money though various means which we put into an endowment," explains Naomi. "Now every year the *shul* uses the interest to support small charities in Israel and locally." Danny was impressed with the work that Naomi had done in her own congregation, and the two became friends.

About a year later, Danny (who lives in Silver Springs, MD) asked Naomi to volunteer twelve to fifteen hours weekly to his Ziv Foundation. "I considered this an incredible honor," remembers Naomi. "It was at about this same time that I was diagnosed with breast cancer. It may sound strange when I say it, but the cancer may have been one of the best things that ever happened to me. It put my priorities in line. I realized that a lot of things are important and a lot of other things are not. I went through many unpleasant treatments, but the work I was doing for Ziv gave me the boost I needed to get through it. What I was learning was a really powerful message. The more *mitzvot* I did the more I wanted to do. Doing one *mitzvah* makes you do another."

In any case, the twelve hours a week was really upwards of twenty. Because Naomi was now an active part of Ziv, the organization grew. She was the one available to take phone calls and answer email. Naomi was the person who wrote the grants. Danny Siegel says, "I would have closed the fund if Naomi hadn't come to work. I needed someone to run it on a day-to-day basis when I was on the road speaking and educating." Ziv exploded from a fund that gave out 250,000 dollars per year to one that will give three quarters of a million this year. "This is not work," says Naomi. "It's the most exciting thing I could do with my life. It's life affirming. I am blessed to do God's work." Eventually, Naomi became a paid full-time administrator of Ziv, which boasts only using ten percent of the donations to cover its expenses.

What is Ziv exactly? Ziv is a registered nonprofit organization that is dedicated to the collection and distribution of money to little known, grassroots *tzedakah* projects. It provides financial support to organizations that offer direct, significant and immediate services with a minimum of overhead and bureaucracy. For example, Ziv is one of the main financial supporters of a small organization in Israel called Amuta for the Support of Fiancees. "We discovered this organization last spring. It was started back in 1997 by Phyllis Heimowitz," says Naomi. "One *motzei* Shabbos back in 1997, Phyllis' daughter, Michal was supposed to become engaged to Lt. Avi Booker, *z"l*, who was then stationed in Lebanon. Lt. Booker never placed the ring on Michal's finger, because he was killed in the line of duty that week. Michal was devastated. Her personality and demeanor changed. Her family was terribly worried about her and they had no where to turn. The government had all sorts of therapy programs available for relatives of fallen soldiers, but nothing for fiancees." After months of advocating to get help for Michal and others in her situation, Phyllis and her other daughter, Tamar, finally convinced the IDF to provide a small stipend to form an organization to help these young women. However, Phyllis and Tamar were on their own in terms of how to develop and run such a project. "We learned of their group from an email from one of Phyllis' nieces," explains Naomi. "We've since given them thousands of dollars to expand their programs. Sadly, the group has grown from one weekly therapy group to eleven because of all the casualties of this current war. Now there is even a support group for men who were engaged to fallen female soldiers. To me, this is an outstanding example of what we do. Our money is directly concentrated in terms of direct aid."

During the course of any given day, Naomi writes checks, speaks to donors on the telephone and answers email. She spends countless hours advising the volunteers of the small organizations that Ziv supports on how to effectively get themselves up and running. "You have to remember," explains Naomi, "these are people with terrific ideas who want to repair the world. However, not too many of them know a great deal about how to run an organization. I offer them the support that they need."

Ziv also is the number one resource for individuals who want to pair their *simcha* with a *mitzvah* project. A bar mitzvah boy named Donni Engelhart from Chicago contacted Ziv when he thought of an incredibly inventive project to undertake at his *simcha*. Naomi helped him to put his idea into motion. Donni asked the guests to bring their old sheitels to his reception. Then, he collected them all, and donated them to an organization called, "Y Me," which cares for cancer patients. "There is no limit to what can be done," enthuses Naomi, "the only limit is our own imaginations."

For years, Ziv has been providing funds to Clara Hammer, otherwise known as the Chicken Lady of Jerusalem. Every week, Clara, who is now an astounding ninety-three years old, arranges for Mr. Hacker, the butcher, to provide two chickens and a half a kilo of chopped meat to families in need. At present, Clara is collecting money and distributing chickens to some 200 hungry Jewish families. Meanwhile, back in America, Ziv is working to find individuals and groups to help *mitzvah* heroes like Clara. Naomi made a connection between a high school class in Baltimore with Clara. These American kids wanted to begin on a *tzedakah* project during their freshman year, and then on their senior class trip to Israel, they wanted to deliver the fruits of their labors. Unfortunately, their trip to Israel was canceled. However, just this month, their principal traveled to Jerusalem and presented Clara with a check from the children for $8,500. A small miracle.

"In the years ahead," says Naomi, "I hope that Ziv will continue to grow." Each day when Danny is on the road speaking or in his office writing, Naomi is making sure the wheels of Ziv keep turning. "Nothing could make me happier than continuing to do this job," confesses Naomi. "Every day, I get to save a life or two – literally. How many people get to say that?"

Jenny Kaplan, *z"l*°

An Angel Who Left Too Soon

When Judah Kaplan remembers his late wife, Jenny, he frequently says the same thing, "she was not about to allow a minor, insignificant thing like cancer to stop her from living life." And it didn't. Studying photographs of Jenny, it was clear to see that she was a young woman who embraced life, who smiled not only with her lips, but as Judah says, "also with her eyes." "Recently, I watched the video of our wedding" wistfully recalls Judah, "and we were both so happy, we were shining."

But when life threw the couple some unexpected curve balls, like Jenny's Hodgkin's disease diagnosis in May 2000, they remained optimistic. "This is the 'good' cancer," explains Judah, "the doctors told us that there was more than an 80% chance that she would be cured." Jenny and Judah viewed this disease as a bump in the road and they fully expected to lead a long and healthy life together.

What was truly amazing about Jenny was that even during her cancer treatments she continued to do for others. She was involved in the Sisterhood of the Young Israel of Teaneck, NJ. She was the Vice President for fund raising and organized wine sales and boutiques. If something needed to be done, people gave the job to Jenny. This devoted young wife, sister, sister-in-law, daughter and career woman was the type of person who made lists. She even made lists for other people, especially her husband, in an attempt to keep his life on track and on schedule. "I didn't even open the mail. Jenny loved to pay all of the bills. She loved to get things done. The only thing Jenny liked more than making lists" quips Judah "was crossing

---

° Permission given by husband.

things off." Jenny was a wife and also social secretary for Judah, and she liked it that way.

Jenny was an accomplished young woman. She graduated from Barnard after studying for a year at Midreshet Moriah (a women's yeshiva seminary in Israel). Then Jenny went on to earn an MBA from Columbia Business School and the final feather in her cap was when she became a Chartered Financial Analyst (CFA). She held down a full-time job at Wyeth Consumer Health as the Associate Brand Manager for Centrum Kids© and more recently, Advil©. When Jenny had to miss one day a week of work for chemotherapy, her boss never complained. He said that, "Jenny could do in four days what other people could do in seven."

Judah and Jenny thought they had their entire lives ahead of them in September of 2000 when Jenny completed radiation therapy and was pronounced "cured." They began an extensive remodeling job on their home, with Jenny acting as director for the project. She had a particular vision of what everything would look like and loved seeing her ideas come to fruition. But, the most important task of Jenny's young life lay before her. After the *Yom Tovim* in 2001, a family donated a *Sefer Torah* to The Young Israel of Teaneck. The last four lines of the scroll were written but not filled in by the *sofer*. Jenny took on the responsibility of organizing a drive to sell the final letters in the Torah in order to raise funds for her *shul*. The Young Israel of Teaneck is bursting at the seams with more and more young children each *Shabbat*. Jenny loved being around them. She delighted in the growth of her community. Therefore, when the town granted their approval for the congregation to build a larger building, Jenny dove in to raise the money.

However, in October of 2001, Jenny felt another ominous lump. In a characteristically unselfish act, she didn't tell Judah about her discovery until the next day, because she didn't want to spoil his birthday. Several weeks later, Jenny was diagnosed with a recurrence. But, that didn't stop her from working just as hard to complete the *Sefer Torah*. Jenny only confided in those closest to her about her illness. In the end, she raised over 7,000 dollars for the *shul*. "On the day of the Torah dedication she couldn't lift her arm," remembers Judah. "She was in a lot of pain – and we weren't sure why. Nonetheless, with her arm in a sling, she was busy directing traffic. A week later she had surgery to remove a blood clot in that arm."

Finally, once again, Jenny was pronounced healthy. The relieved and overjoyed young couple decided to take a vacation to California to relax and to celebrate. In the evening at about five forty-five, just as she was about to serve dinner, Jenny turned to Judah and told him that she wasn't feeling well. As he held her, she collapsed in his arms. Less than one and a half hours later, Jenny was pronounced dead.

Judah eulogized his young wife and his best friend. He spoke about how Jenny maintained friendships from elementary school, high school, college, camp and Israel. She had Jewish friends and non-Jewish friends. "Jenny's life was like a train ride. She picked up friends at every stop, and nobody wanted to get off the train," says Judah. One of Jenny's closest relationships was with her sister, Justine. Jenny was always so proud of her sister. She frequently talked about how she believed that some day, Justine, a researcher in neurobiology, would win the Nobel Prize.

Jenny had a loving relationship with her parents, William and Cynthia Levin of Chicago. Her father, in an act of pure unselfishness, helped Judah with the incredibly painful task of making his own daughter's funeral arrangements. In the months since her death, his parents and Jenny's parents have showed Judah a tremendous amount of love and support in the face of their own grief. Judah's siblings and their spouses and Jenny's sister are with Judah every step of the way for emotional support. Jenny is sorely missed by all of them.

However, Jenny and Judah always believed that God has a master plan and that there is a reason for everything. Judah believes that he may never understand the reason for Jenny's death, or he may only understand it many years from now. But, until then, Judah finds his faith in God's infinite wisdom a great source of comfort.

Eileen Sklaroff

Helping the Poor Among Us

Ask Eileen Sklaroff for a tour of the offices of the Female Hebrew Benevolent Society (FHBS) and she'll invite you to her see her home and ask you to stay for dinner. That's because this organization, which was founded in 1819, is committed to raising money for poor Jewish women in the Philadelphia area with a minimal amount of overhead. In fact, under Eileen's steady leadership, annual dollars raised now top $10,000.

Who is Eileen and what is the FHBS? Eighteen-nineteen was a particularly cold and harsh winter in Philadelphia. Hannah Levy and Mrs. Aaron Levy, members of Mikveh Israel (the third oldest congregation in America) learned that there were poor Jewish women in their midst. The two Levys were shocked that some women didn't even have firewood to heat their homes. They were further dismayed to discover that there was no Jewish communal organization in Philadelphia to help these people. Sadly, only Christian missionary groups were available to lend a hand – but not without a dose of proselytizing included.

It was then that the FHBS was founded by these women as a Jewish response to poverty. Quickly, they drafted Rebecca Gratz as their first secretary. The philosophy of the organization was shaped by her eloquent writing. The new society divided the city into quadrants and found out what was needed in Jewish households. Then, they did what needed to be done. If a particular family needed meals, then the FHBS cooked them. If a family needed a bill to be paid, the FHBS did that as well.

"What is significant about the FHBS," says Eileen, "is that it is the first community organization founded by Jews to help Jews in Philadelphia.

And it is the oldest Jewish charitable organization in continuous operation in the United States." The FHBS doesn't visit homes any more. Most referrals come through social workers. The vast majority of the women need something immediate; payment of rent, a mortgage or a utility bill. "Sometimes we even buy supermarket certificates for our clients," explains Eileen, "and we give out many camp scholarships and have even paid for gravestones." Basically, the FHBS steps in and fills a need wherever they see one.

Among others, the clients of the FHBS are victims of domestic violence, single mothers, widows who are the sole support of young children and women with chronic illnesses. Most of these women are living on some sort of public entitlement, yet, sometimes that money is not enough. An emergency arises, and the FHBS steps in.

None of these acts of *chesed* would be possible without the leadership of Eileen Sklaroff. It is she who volunteers upwards of twenty hours a week on tasks such as handling correspondence, paying bills, writing thank you notes, developing grant proposals, doing telephone intakes with clients and soliciting funds. "In Philadelphia, there are a disproportionate number of Jewish poor. Across the board it is a working-class city," says Eileen. "Jews are no exception. They are undereducated and underemployed. In the Book of *Devarim*, God tells us that there will always be poor among us and that it is our responsibility to help them. So, I don't feel as if it's our job to eradicate poverty – but to help those in need, with sensitivity, caring and respect. We need to make it as easy as possible for our clients to get help while preserving their dignity."

How did a nice, upper middle class Jewish woman become involved in helping the most needy in her community? About fifteen years ago, Eileen received a telephone call from Mrs. Bert Braude, the widow of her maternal grandmother's first cousin. The Braude's and Eileen's grandparents lived in the same West Philadelphia neighborhood as newlyweds and maintained a friendship throughout their lives. Mrs. Braude had been a particularly good friend to Eileen's grandmother, especially when she became ill and needed to be placed in a nursing home. Thus, when Mrs. Braude asked Eileen to attend a meeting and become a board member of the FHBS, she couldn't refuse.

"I didn't want to be involved in this," recalls Eileen. "I was busy raising my kids and volunteering at their schools. But I just couldn't say 'no.' When I arrived at the first meeting, it felt pretty weird. The women were all very formal. They were wearing hats and white gloves. I was only in my mid-thirties and they were all in the their seventies and eighties." At first, Eileen's involvement was only peripheral. But then, a year and a half after her first meeting, Mrs. Braude announced to Eileen that she was the new treasurer.

Then sadly, Mrs. Braude's mental and physical health began to decline. "I called her daughter, Ruth," remembers Eileen, "and asked her if we could make her mother a president emeritus. Ruth agreed and decided to become involved on the board in her mother's place. Mrs. Vera Bloomfield, herself in her eighties, took over the role of president. Then about fourteen years ago, Mrs. Bloomfield arrived at an FHBS meeting with a letter for Eileen written on a piece of crisp, white monogrammed stationary. In it, she explained to Eileen that it was now her turn to take over the reigns of the FHBS. Since that time, Eileen has lived and breathed the FHBS.

"It is my privilege to be able to do this and bring it to this level of giving. I am honored to guide and develop this organization. I've learned not to be judgmental and to just do the work. It feels great to perpetuate a tradition that is 186 years old," waxes Eileen. "It's also a good feeling to be part of something where other Jewish agencies work together. None of us cares what denomination the women belong to – as long as they are Jewish and need our help."

Section 3

Hachnasat Orchim / Hospitality

Hospitality is one form of worship.
unknown

The next time you want to invite a bunch of friends over, you might convince (and definitely impress) your mother by telling her that having company is a Jewish thing to do. Opening of one's home to guests is a tradition that dates back to the first Hebrew couple, Abraham and Sarah. In Genesis (18:4), we learn that they graciously welcomed lodgers into their tent: "Let now a little water be fetched, and wash your feet, and recline yourselves under a tree."

Later in Genesis, God destroys the cities of Sodom and Gomorrah because of the wickedness of their inhabitants. One of their worst sins was the manner in which they treated strangers. The following legend is recounted in commentaries on the Torah portion, *V'Yairah*, "A girl overcome by pity supplied food to a poor stranger. On detection, she was stripped, bound, daubed with honey and placed on the roof under the burning sun to be devoured by bees."

The value of welcoming visitors was underscored during the Talmudic era, "Hospitality to strangers shows reverence for the name of the Lord." (BT, Sabbath 127a). In Pirkei Avot (1:5), it states, "Let your houses be wide open, always treating the poor as members of your own family." In modern times, the legacy of extending oneself to newcomers continues. In the aftermath of the Nazi Holocaust, Jewish women opened their homes to survivors until they were resettled.

More recently, communities and individuals have been instrumental in assimilating Jewish immigrants from the former Soviet Union, Arab Nations and Ethiopia. In the United States, Jewish Federations, Hebrew Day Schools, *yeshivot*, synagogues and Jewish community centers welcomed these individuals, and throughout America many have been included in family functions such as *Shabbat* dinners, Passover Seders and *B'nei Mitzvah*.

Perhaps it is because Jews have been wanderers throughout most of our 3,000 year old history that Jewish women empathize with and are anxious to offer comfort to the traveler. In fact the Torah commands us: "to be kind to the stranger because you were strangers in Egypt." Many Jewish women make this *mitzvah* a cornerstone of their lives; touching all those who enter their homes.

Bessie Fishman Newell, *z"l* and Rachel Bess Levine

Up in Heaven Smiling

If I slept at my grandma's house on any given Thursday night, I would wake up Friday morning to find huge ceramic bowls, filled with *challah* dough, covered with checkered dishcloths sitting on the radiator; cinnamon buns dotted with raisins and laced with sugar rising on the counter; garlic sticks, slathered with olive oil and salt, lined up on trays next to the stove; and loaf pans filled with molasses cake batter already baking in the oven. Often, my Grandma would be peeling apples or rolling out the crust for pie that even now, if I close my eyes and concentrate, I can still taste. All the while, her hands were dancing in a seemingly effortless ballet, gliding from task to task, without recipes, food processors or microwave ovens.

My Grandma Bessie was exotic, with haunting dark eyes and shiny jet black hair set against creamy white skin. Her disposition was as fiery (though some thought her abrasive) as her appearance. At seventeen, she married Eli Newell who brought her, somewhat unwillingly, from Philadelphia to Cohoes, New York, a tiny and isolated mill town upstate.

Grandma was an enigma. She had hands that worked incredibly hard, yet retained their softness. She had no formal schooling, yet she could do things that nobody else I knew could. There was nothing she could not accomplish with a needle and thread. As I sat mesmerized next to her rocking chair, she would produce a dress for my Barbie doll in any color or style I wanted. But her most amazing feats were achieved in the kitchen. Every Friday morning, she would awaken before sunrise and begin the process of baking for *Shabbat*.

In the midst of her baking, she would give me some dough to "work" and tell me some *bubbamissas* (old wives' tales) that I could not, despite my best efforts, erase from my mind. For example, she would say, "Debby, don't ever eat chocolate ice cream, only vanilla, because chocolate ice cream is brown and they hide things in it." Or, "pinch your nose one hundred times a day and train it to be skinny." I would ask her again and again to show me how to prepare even one of her concoctions, and she always flatly refused. "I don't want you to be an old pot scrubber like me. You're smart, don't spend your time at the stove, get an education," my Grandmother would admonish. And yet, she always carried out her duties with dignity and pride. Grandma considered baking her work and I, her naïve but willing accomplice, thought her work immensely important. Strangely, I never wondered why Grandma would go to such great lengths to prepare these delicacies for such a small family: my uncle, my parents, my sister and me. But on Friday you would have thought she had scores of relatives. As morning turned into afternoon, one masterpiece after another would be completed, filling her house with an intoxicating aroma. Slowly, a steady stream of visitors would almost magically appear at her door – including the insurance man, the milkman, the grocer across the street, the landlady, neighborhood kids and the dry cleaner. An eclectic mix paraded through my Grandmother's kitchen each Friday afternoon. She made conversation with each and never allowed anyone to leave "without a little something."

Did Grandma Bessie welcome guests to her house because it was a Jewish value? Did inviting people make her home more Jewish? I'm not sure. But I do know that baking was reserved for Friday, for *erev Shabbat*. I vividly recall her tearing off a piece of *challah* dough before she began baking, reciting a *b'racha* (a blessing) and then discarding it. She put her own theological spin on this custom by teaching me that the ripping of the *challah* was to remind us of less fortunate people who didn't have enough to eat. She transformed baking *challah* into a ritual. Then, finally when the kitchen was clean, she would tenderly throw a white tablecloth on the kitchen table and *bench licht* (light Sabbath candles).

Grandpa Eli brought her to, as she called it, a "God forsaken place." But I think what she probably meant was that she had to live away from her family and her old Jewish neighborhood. She and Grandpa were part of the tiny Jewish population in their small city and I can only guess that, in some way, Grandma's baking and feeding strangers was her way of bringing Judaism along with her.

My Grandmother died when I was thirteen years old, after spending the last year of her life in a nursing home. I really didn't have her for a very long time. When I cook during the week, I seldom think about her. But, when I'm preparing for *Shabbat* or for *Yom Tov* (festivals), there are those moments when I feel as though she is peering approvingly over my shoulder. I always make that "little extra" in case someone drops by. Somehow, I manage to whip up many dishes at the same time, something I never do Monday through Thursday. Although I am not nearly as adroit as she, I prepare foods specifically so they will have the aroma of *Shabbat*. I want my children to anticipate its approaching from the lovely smells that only homemade goodies can engender. My home is open to friends and family, as well as the guy who bought my used Toyota, the acquaintance who is going through a divorce, kids galore and an autistic neighbor.

My firstborn, Rachel Bess, was born eight years after my Grandmother's death. She was given the middle name "Bess" in memory of my incorrigible, irascible Grandma. Rachel made her entrance into the world colicky, kicking and screaming, and in heaven stole Grandma's coal black eyes, jet black hair and contrary nature. Rachel Bess grew from a baby into a college girl in what seemed like moments. And now, she calls me on the phone to say, "Mommy...I'm making *Shabbat* dinner for fifteen people, do you have a good recipe for chicken cutlets?" Guests in the double digits don't intimidate or deter her. A shortage of space, utensils and appliances is irrelevant to my Rachel Bess. She invites the kid from another college who has no place to go for *Shabbat*, the one who is studying to be an actuary and is a bit antisocial, roommates and friends and, basically, anyone who crosses her path. Yes, she made Dean's list and earned an A in anatomy. She has a life outside of the kitchen, of which I am tremendously proud. But what does she brag about? "I made such a delicious *Shabbat* dinner. I invited six people, but then at the last minute, three more showed up. We had such a great time." Little Rachel Bess, a five-foot-two inch dynamo. Grandma Bessie must be up in heaven, *kvelling.*

Sylvia Ruskin

Shalom Y'All

At seventy plus years old, Sylvia Ruskin is practically an institution in the small Jewish community of Nashville, Tennessee. "I was born in Nashville and my mother was born in Nashville, and although we were surrounded by gentiles, I was always comfortable with my Judaism. Every year the Donovan family would invite us over to look at their Christmas tree. It was really beautiful, but I didn't feel any envy because I was comfortable with who I was," says Sylvia. "To me, part of being Jewish means being involved. In a small town, you have to take more responsibility."

Always active in the Jewish community, Sylvia has been president of Hadassah and of Jewish Family Services. She was instrumental in resettling Russian families in Nashville, helping them find jobs, housing and furniture. "I rented a store house," says Sylvia, "and got people to donate furniture and we kept it in there until a new family came to town. If we couldn't find them what they needed, we would buy it for them. When they first arrived, I would always make sure there was chicken, cabbage, soup, potatoes and carrots in their refrigerators. We became friends – I was there for them and they were there for me."

One activity that has been a favorite of Sylvia's for thirty years has been welcoming new Jewish families to the city of which she is so proud. "I get a new members list from the Jewish Federation and the other Jewish organizations," explains Sylvia in her delightful Southern drawl. "Then I call them on the telephone and welcome them to town and find out who they are. I say, what brings you all to Nashville? Do you have family here? I love finding out who is related to whom. I assure them that I'm not selling anything – that I just love talking to newcomers."

Sometimes Sylvia becomes friends with the newcomers but, she says, "Sometimes the chemistry isn't there, so I match them up with other folks because I know everyone in town. Sometimes people want me to recommend a doctor, or a podiatrist or a beauty salon. This is a friendly city, and people are more than willing to invite a new person over. I just make the connections for them. It's exciting and fun meeting new people. Sometimes I get thank-you notes from them telling me that my call meant a lot to them."

Remembering her adolescence, Sylvia knows how she became open to the idea of welcoming guests. "During World War II, my parents would invite Jewish soldiers from nearby Fort Campbell in Kentucky to eat at our house. I recall two guys, Rappaport and Lerner, and my mother would cook for them all the time," she says. "Then my parents would send them back to the base with a salami. I also remember men coming to our *shul* (synagogue) with a *pushke* (*tzedakah* box) asking for money and my father would always invite them over to our house and give them a donation. I guess taking care of other Jews is in my blood."

Wendy Kay

Shabbat at the Kays

Wendy Kay wasn't always observant. In fact, she never even went to Hebrew School. But, when her first son, Michael, was five-years old, she decided that he needed to learn more about Judaism than she had. So, off the little guy went to the Hebrew Academy in Albany, New York. Wendy never imagined how that decision would change her life.

Michael is now twenty-three years old, a married man pursuing a PhD in Jewish Studies. He was followed by brother Jason and sister Sarah, both involved in their respective Jewish communities.

And Wendy? Over the years, she's learned. First about *kashrut*. Years ago she gave up some of her favorites, bacon and eggs and cheeseburgers. She donated every dish and every pot to charity and made a kosher home. Later, she began to learn about *Shabbat*. Over time, Wendy became more and more observant.

But there's more to Wendy's story. Wendy lives in a big house near a couple of *shuls*. When her kids became teenagers, Wendy encouraged them to bring kids home for *Shabbat* lunch and stay for the afternoon. At first, each of her children would bring a guest. Then, maybe they would each invite two guests. Little by little, "going to the Kays" on *Shabbat* afternoon became a ritual for literally any teenager in Albany. "Going to the Kays" was something that just evolved. Kids who had no place to go on *Shabbat* afternoon (maybe because their parent's were at the mall or at work) could come to the Kays. Kids who were going through a rough time at home could come to the Kays. Or kids who just wanted a hot game of Trivial Pursuit could come to the Kays.

Every Thursday, Wendy would make pans of food for whomever would show up on her doorstep on *Shabbat* afternoon. She always seemed to have more than enough for everyone. Wendy would always whip up a batch of "Wendy cookies" a favorite of all the kids (she still ships batches of them off to college). Some weeks, Wendy would make herself scarce when the kids came over, hibernating in her room with a good book. Inevitably, that didn't last long. One teenager or another would find their way up to her room just to sit at the foot of her bed and talk. Wendy was always a good ear. She talked to them about all kinds of life choices; from selecting a mate to selecting a college.

When Wendy went through a bad divorce, *Shabbat* at the Kays offered her a great deal of solace. Having the kids around gave her comfort. She claims that they gave her more than she gave them – but that's because in her own modest way, she underestimates the affect she's had on so many teenagers.

Now, *Shabbat* at the Kays is not the same as it was before. Her kids are all living out of town and it's pretty quiet on Milner Avenue. However, this summer, Michael will return to Albany to be the director of a local Jewish summer camp. Jason will run the music program and Sarah will teach Israeli dance. As soon as they unpack their suitcases, every teenager in town will somehow know that they've arrived. Undoubtedly, they'll also know that Wendy is busily preparing some goodies to eat and opening her heart and home for their visits. *Shabbat* at the Kays will begin again and last only for June, July and August. But, for a brief moment in time, Wendy will be able to once again give her love to the kids that have always meant so much to her.

Section 4

Bikkur Chollim / Visiting the Sick

If you have ever visited a sick friend or relative in the hospital then you have performed a *mitzvah*. The concept of *bikkur chollim* (visiting the sick) can be traced back to the Book of Genesis, the first book of the Torah. While Abraham was recuperating from his circumcision, God materialized: "And the Lord appeared unto him in the plains of Mamre." Our sages believe that God attended to Abraham during his recuperation as a deed of loving-kindness. The fact that God personally visited Abraham serves to emphasize the significance of this act since Jews are supposed to emulate God by "walking in His ways."

Sometimes people are not sure how to behave when they visit the sick. The *Shulchan Aruch* (Code of Jewish Law) offers some guidelines. These laws suggest compassion, sensitivity and delicacy, "Relatives and friends who are accustomed to visiting someone often, should visit him or her as soon as they hear of a sickness. But strangers should not call immediately, but wait three days, in order not to spoil the chances of recovery by defining the person as a patient. If, however, someone suddenly becomes ill, even a stranger should visit him immediately. Even a great man should visit a less important person, and even many times during the day. It is meritorious to visit a sick person as frequently as possible, providing it does not weary the sick individual" (Shulchan Aruch 193:1).

Often, Jewish women visit nursing homes and hospitals, bringing hope and comfort to patients. As you will see, some carry out their work in innovative ways. The women profiled in this section take care of the ill in a variety of settings and their Jewish values guide them in their efforts.

Barbara Sarah

Pain is Inevitable – Suffering is Optional

"When we visit breast cancer patients, we create healing events," says Barbara Sarah. "Usually five or six members of our Healing Circle Improvisation Group show up for each visit and we bring the patient healing wishes. First we introduce ourselves, then we allow the patient to talk about her own concerns and needs. We stand around the bed and all hold hands and spend a few minutes in quiet. Then we see what part of her story touches us. We pass a squeeze around the circle and then we spring into action. Sometimes we sing; sometimes we are prayerful; we might touch her or stroke her head, depending on what she needs. We do whatever seems appropriate. Women love this. They need the attention, they need to feel loved."

Barbara is a social worker at the Fern Feldman Anolick Breast Center in Kingston, New York. Her approach in dealing with her own disease and the illnesses of others is summarized in one statement: "Pain is inevitable, suffering is optional." Barbara's approach involves lots of outdoor activities as well as arts and crafts. I don't run a standard support group where we all sit around and talk about our feelings. We go canoeing, white water rafting, or fly fishing. We garden, create artwork and participate in educational programs. One woman recently said to me that if she hadn't gotten breast cancer she wouldn't have been able to do all of these things." Barbara subscribes to an alternative mental health philosophy called Constructive Living. She explains, "Constructive Living does not attempt to alter how one feels. It influences one's behavior and, hopefully, in turn, that changes one's feelings in a positive way. I try to give people hope. I try to help them enrich their lives no matter how much or how little time they have left." Barbara composed a poem which captures these sentiments:

Sacred and scared are close in this circle of women
Celebrating each other, themselves and life.
Coming together in uncertainty
Feeling the pain in the back, the lung, the head:
A passing distraction or a signal of recurrence?
Pay attention, dear friends:
The fear of death contains the fear of life.
Go to the garden. Hike in the rain.
Create a patch for a quilt.
Sing, swim, try sacred dance.
Cook healing soup. Stretch, grow and learn.
Touch and be touched in this precious time of Now.

"The other pillar of my work is Judaism. As a kid I was sent to a Jewish camp," she recalls. I found myself there. I discovered I had leadership abilities. I learned a lot about our tradition, which teaches us that life is sacred. When we wake up in the morning, we say a blessing thanking God that we're alive. We are supposed to notice and appreciate what we've been given. When you get breast cancer, people are very generous. I remember that when I was sick my three daughters came into my hospital room like angels. They are busy with their own lives and it's not every day that they get together, but they came to support me. And there is a lot you get from other people too – each and every day. I take notice of those things and I am thankful for them."

The job that Barbara does is sometimes difficult and heartbreaking. She explains, "I keep doing this work because people I have come to love have died. I was able to help support them through the process. This work is a good balance of dealing with dying people and enriching people by bringing out their creativity. I help empower women so they can participate in their own recoveries."

Zella Goldfinger and Chava Rose

A Hidden Agenda

Recently, two women were staying at one of the Lenox Hill *Bikkur Chollim*'s Hospitality apartments. One was not observant and the other was ultra-Orthodox. Each had a gravely-ill husband. If it were not for their husbands' illnesses, the life paths of these individuals probably would not have crossed. After a few days of living together in one of the apartments, they began to share their sleepless, anxiety-filled nights talking and deriving comfort and companionship from one another. Each learned that the other was terrified of widowhood and spending the remainder of her life alone. The preconceptions with which each woman regarded the other melted away as they poured out their hearts, shared their fears, and comforted each other. They weathered a terrifying storm together. And, although they have returned to their respective communities, these women maintain frequent telephone contact.

Zella Goldfinger and Chava Rose are the two full-time volunteers who run three such apartments in the fashionable Lenox Hill section of Manhattan. "The *Bikkur Chollim* apartments are an opportunity to tear down walls and build bridges within the Jewish community," says Zella. "During the past year, the *Bikkur Chollim* apartments have hosted almost 2,000 overnight stays, accommodating, at no charge, families of patients at many local hospitals including Lenox Hill, Memorial Sloan-Kettering, New York University and Mount Sinai. We try to provide a comfortable, pleasant place for people who are sometimes far from home and dealing with a loved one's serious illness. Having a place to stay that is convenient to the hospital, clean, quiet and free of charge, alleviates some of the stress faced by patients' family members."

Each apartment is clean, cozy, and comfortable. They are stocked with linens towels and blankets, all of which have been donated. The kitchen is "*Shabbat* ready" with candlesticks, candles, grape juice, *kiddush* cups in the cupboards and *challah* and chicken soup in the freezer. Zelda and Chava oversee the apartments' maintenance, and work at keeping them attractive and inviting. They also raise the funds to pay the hefty rent bills due each month. "Our purpose in performing this *mitzvah* appears obvious: to provide comfort to the sick and their families," Chava explains. "Yet, there is much more here than meets the eye. Though on one level we are in the business of *Bikkur Chollim*, on a deeper level, we are really fostering the love between Jews – *ahavat yisrael*. This happens when our volunteers (who represent the spectrum of Jewish affiliation) visit patients (who also represent this spectrum). It also happens when Jewish people who express their Judaism quite differently share the experience of the illness of a loved one. The barriers dissolve as our guests help and encourage one another. The ability to relate to other Jews with love, understanding, compassion and tolerance is a natural outgrowth of our work." Zella and Chava consciously capitalize on every opportunity to help Jews communicate with and be supportive of other Jews in their hospitality facilities.

Beyond their involvement with the apartments, these women train volunteers, both teenage and adult, to visit the sick at Lenox Hill Hospital. In one recent year, Zella, Chava and their *Bikkur Chollim* Volunteers paid over 15,000 visits. "It's amazing to see Reform teenagers, dressed in blue jeans, visiting Chasidic patients wearing black velvet *kippot,*" Zella comments. "Again, two groups of people who ordinarily would not meet, but under these circumstances, they share a common goal – the recovery and comfort of the patient – that connects them. Some of these teens have gone on to college and organized their own *bikkur chollim* groups. Others come back during school vacations to visit patients at Lenox Hill Hospital."

In the spring of 1987, Chava visited a hospitalized woman who had survived Auschwitz and who was battling cancer. "While I was sitting at her bed-side, I realized that the overworked staff could not possibly spare the time to sit with patients, listen to their life stories, be there to hold a hand when they expressed their fears and anxieties." She began to visit patients on a regular basis. Shortly after that, Chava met Zella in a Hebrew language class and Zella joined Chava in her efforts. Zella recalls, "There was something so right, so pure, so genuine in what Chava was doing that I couldn't resist."

The duo are anxious to take the focus off themselves and acknowledge their scores of assistants. Zella explains, "We feel there is a reason that we have never had to actively recruit help; the phenomenal volunteers are God's reward for our efforts. Although we are exposed to immeasurable suffering and anguish, we also see extraordinary heroism in patients and their families and incredible good in the accomplishments of our volunteers. We are inspired by both the patients whom we meet and our volunteers!"

Zella says, "There is no ego, nothing political, in what we do. Everyone in the organization does whatever needs to be done...bringing something to a hospital patient, cleaning the apartments for Passover, helping with a fund-raising mailing. We consider it all a part of doing *bikkur chollim*. You can condense all of Judaism into *bikkur chollim* and the way you treat people. *Bikkur Chollim* embraces the tenets of a Torah life."

Joan Posnick

Living for Others

Losing a baby during a pregnancy or in early infancy is a death. It's a death of a dream, the death of potential, the death of an already much loved family member, and the death of a future for that particular child.

No matter how many more children a couple is blessed with following a miscarriage, no child will ever take the place of the lost baby in the parents' hearts and minds. So why then, as a society, are we sometimes so callous and thoughtless when we speak to a grieving mother or father? Why do people utter worlds like, "don't worry, you'll have more children," "just try again," or even "it's better this way"? The answer, according to Joan Posnick, is that people don't mean to be hurtful, but they are uneducated. Quite simply, the only appropriate thing to say is, "I'm sorry."

Joan knows of what she speaks. Many years ago, this mother of three healthy children, Yonatan, Avi and Chana, experienced two tragedies. She and her husband, Jerry, lost one child after sixteen days of life, and another to a miscarriage at five months. Once during kiddush, someone approached her and said, "Better luck next time."

Joan's children describe her in the following way, "our Mom is trying to help other women and at the same time trying to educate the public about how to behave in these situations. Her sons and daughter refer to her work as *tikkun olam* – repair of the world.

As her own children understand, Joan Posnick is not one to allow her own misfortune to stop her from helping others. Rather, she attempts to imbue meaning into her experiences by caring for others in the same or similar situation. That's why besides teaching Spanish full-time in a yeshiva, she spends time volunteering. "Personally, I believe that everything is *bashert* (preordained/fated), and it was God's plan for me to help these people."

When a woman suffers the death of an infant or a miscarriage, she can call the National Council for Jewish Women's Pregnancy Loss Support Program. The woman will be asked a variety of questions, and then matched with a counselor. Joan is one of the giving individuals who spend countless hours helping these young women deal with their loss. Over the past fifteen years, Joan has counseled over 300 women.

"The first thing I do for these women is say, 'I'm sorry.' By saying these words, I validate their loss," explains Joan. Then Joan asks these women to tell her about what they've gone through because before they can work though the pain, they need to grieve. They need to talk. In addition, Joan tells these women that although people say many hurtful things in this type of situation, they generally don't mean to inflict harm.

Joan talks about how she still personally experiences this type of insensitivity and ignorance. She displays a picture of her son, Joshua, *z"l*, among her family photographs. When asked how she can keep a picture of a deceased baby on her wall, she is stunned by the question. "After all, I have pictures of my late parents in my home and nobody questions why I would want to look at them," she says. "Joshua was a member of my family and he belongs there."

On a practical level, Joan provides bereaved mothers with advice for getting through their darkest days. For example, when a woman schedules her first post-birth appointment with her obstetrician, Joan recommends that she should try to take the earliest slot possible. This way, the grieving mother doesn't have to sit in an office filled with pregnant women. Joan tells them that anything they are feeling is normal, and that they are not crazy. When people seem to want to rush them into "getting over it," Joan encourages them to take the time they need to grieve.

After the women speak with Joan on the telephone three or four times, they have the option of participating in a couple's group. The husbands are also offered a chance to speak to a male counselor. In some cases, these women contact Joan months or even years later when they become pregnant again. She helps them to deal with the anxieties and fears that so often crop up in such circumstances.

At what moment did Joan know that she was destined to do this kind of *mitzvah*? "When I had living children, I felt that I had to bring some kind of meaning to my loss," recalls Joan. "Parents are not supposed to bury children, it's supposed to be the other way around. This is not something you ever 'get over.' The pain lessens over time. But there are times when the loss is felt more intensely. Joan had an especially rough time during the period when Joshua would have become a bar mitzvah.

"I never could have gotten through this if I didn't believe that God's plan was for me to help these people," says Joan. "I did volunteer work since I was a teenager. I believe that you have to live your life to help other people."

Section 5

V'ahavta L'reyacha Kamocha / Loving One's Neighbor As Oneself

What we get out of life is in direct proportion to what we put into it.
E.R. Murrow, "This I Believe"

Many people don't know this but the "Golden Rule" actually originated in the Torah: "Love your neighbor as yourself, I am God" (Leviticus 19:18). When people talk about this particular commandment, they often omit the verse's final words, "I am God." This three-word clause teaches us that because God created both you and your neighbor, He has the prerogative to tell you how to behave (God is kind of like your mother and father rolled up into one).

The Babylonian Talmud recounts the famous story of Rabbi Hillel that illustrates the centrality of this *mitzvah* to Judaism; "A man comes before the great rabbi and asks him to state what Judaism is all about, very briefly. "Teach me the entire Torah while standing on one foot." Hillel, who lived 2,000 years ago, did not regard the man's question as rude or foolish, and replied: 'What is hateful to yourself do not do to your neighbor. That is the whole Torah. All the rest is commentary. Now go and study.'" Hillel's answer was so appealing to the man, the *Talmud* tells us, that he, a non-Jew, converted to Judaism.

Caring for others within the Jewish community and in the larger world is the heart and soul of the Jewish way of life. Jewish women perform this *mitzvah* in countless ways. Some of their actions are small and others grand, but each has the effect of making someone in their family or community feel cared for and loved.

Eve Stern

He Carries a Blessing into the World

Eve Stern grew up as the third child of a prominent Jewish family in Portland, Oregon. "My parents and older siblings have always been involved in various aspects of communal life," according to Eve. "My father gives his heart, soul, time and money to causes that benefit the Jewish people. I, on the other hand, was a tad rebellious, and had no interest in becoming immersed in my family's ventures and values."

Her greatest desire was to have a happy marriage and to become a mother. "After I married the man I love who is also my best friend, I was thrilled when I discovered that I was pregnant. Becoming Harrison's mother was like the scene in the Wizard of Oz when Dorothy steps out of black and white Kansas and enters the colorful land of Oz," recalls Eve. "I felt that I finally knew what life was about."

However, as Harrison grew, Eve realized that something was terribly wrong. "At eighteen-months, my son knew all of his numbers and letters, but had no social language skills. His pediatrician assured me that he was developing normally and my husband, my family and my friends tried to comfort me by telling me that I was experiencing the anxieties of a first-time mother. But my doubts, which no one else seemed to take seriously, nagged at me day and night," remembers Eve. Finally, at Harrison's three-year checkup, when his language was still limited to mimicking Disney tapes and imitating a few phrases, his physician referred him to a speech pathologist named Bob.

Bob immediately recognized that Harrison was not developing typically and sent him for a more extensive evaluation. He believed that

Harrison might have Pervasive Developmental Disorder (PDD), the mildest form of autism. Eve says, "I finally had validation for my feelings, which was a relief on some level, but at the same time I was devastated by the reality that something so serious could be wrong with my only son." The assessment confirmed Bob's theory. "I was crushed. But I didn't have the luxury of thinking about myself or my own feelings. I began the hectic routine of driving Harrison to speech therapy, sensory integration therapy and language based pre-school classes. When I wasn't taking him to therapies, I was working with him at home," remembers Eve.

Finally, with the whirlwind of Harrison's third and fourth years behind her, he entered kindergarten with his peers. Although he still required the support of a speech pathologist, occupational therapist and psychologist, he had made tremendous gains. It was at that point, when she had a moment to catch her breath, that Eve sank into a horrible depression. "When I was no longer running on automatic pilot, I began to realize the enormity of my situation and withdrew from contact with other people: I crashed and burned," says Eve.

It was in the midst of the emptiest period of her life that she received a telephone call from a friend who was director of the United Jewish Appeal's (UJA) Woman's Division, asking her to chair their fund raising campaign. "I tried to decline her request, protesting that I was incapable. But my friend knew that I was living a nightmare and insisted, encouraging me to believe I was up to the challenge. I knew I had to do something to dig myself out of the hole I was in, or I would never get out. And so I relented. During my two years as chairman, I developed and used leadership skills I never knew I possessed and began to feel as though I was part of the world again. The cloud of depression that hung over me began to lift," says Eve.

"I was lucky to be able to travel to Israel with the UJA and one *erev Shabbat* (Sabbath eve), I was at the *kotel* (Western Wall remnant of the Second Temple) in Jerusalem, listening to beautiful guitar music playing as the city turned golden in the setting sun. Placing my hand on the Wall, I expressed my most fervent prayers and believed that they would be heard. I didn't have a big epiphany," she says, "but I had a moment. In Israel I saw how the money I had raised was being used to fund a group home for adults with developmental disabilities and went home feeling increasingly connected to the Jewish community and proud of the work I had been doing."

"Returning to Portland, I had an even stronger desire to give of myself. Not only did I feel that my contributions were important, but helping others made me feel good. Meaningful work had gotten me through my lowest moments," recalls Eve. "At that point, I allied myself with another mother of a special needs son, and we supported and inspired each other. Through our own experiences and by watching those of others, we realized that the Portland Jewish community was not meeting the needs of families with special needs children." Once again, Eve had significant things to accomplish.

Together, these two women founded an organization called TASK (Treasuring and Accepting our Special Kids). The purpose of TASK is to provide support for families, to develop and set up programming, and to educate the community to become more inclusive. "I believe that if these families feel that their children can be part of organized Jewish life, they themselves will be more inclined to affiliate within the Jewish community," explains Eve. TASK teaches members of Jewish youth groups about people with developmental disabilities. The teenagers in these organizations, in turn, plan numerous activities for the special needs kids. TASK initiated the *Tikvah* (hope) group which targets Jewish young adults with developmental disabilities who are aging out of the educational system and are often floundering, looking for a place to belong. Their eventual goal is to develop a residential program for the members of *Tikvah*. Under the direction of TASK, a local Conservative synagogue has created a Sunday school class, open to the entire Jewish community, for special needs kids who otherwise could never have attended.

Eve says, "TASK continues to be a uniting force within the Portland Jewish community since it helps people understand that there are many different types of Jews, and that we need to make a place for all of them. Harrison is a gift that has made me feel empathy in a way I had never experienced before. And when I felt the most emptiness, Judaism was in there baking, and when I needed it the most, it was there for me."

Myriam Gummerman

A Family of Angels

Myriam Gummerman of Pittsburgh, PA is a woman who seems to have it all; a family that peacefully co-exists, a husband, Lewis, whom she adores and who adores her in return, and a lovely home in a wonderful community. But Myriam and Lewis, who are in their 50s, decided to expand their family – though not in the traditional sense. Rather, they embarked upon the process of sharing their love and good fortune with the Schwob family in Israel.

The story of how these two families became intertwined appears to be *beshert.* "It all began when my brother returned from a solidarity mission to Israel and called to tell us about it," remembers Myriam. "He talked about the poverty in Israel caused by the Intifada. I felt sickened by the images he described of children rummaging around in garbage cans to find food. Children have always been in my heart."

That night, Myriam and Lewis could not sleep and stayed up into the wee hours figuring out how they could help a family in Israel. "I didn't want to go through an organization," explains Myriam, "I wanted to do something more personal."

Myriam asked her friends, Gene and Ellen Sukov, who spend half of each year in Israel, to see what they could do about connecting her with a family in need. The Sukovs put Myriam in touch with Mark Pollack, a native of Pittsburgh, who had made *aliyah* (immigrated to Israel) several years earlier. This was the beginning of a beautiful collaboration.

Mark Pollack worked with a certain Mrs. Schwob in Israel. Mrs. Schwob told him about her son and his family's situation. Mark was so moved that he was already trying to help them himself – sending them money and giving them moral support whenever he could. Thus, when he received the request from the Gummermans via the Sukovs – he made the match. Clearly, some matches are made in heaven.

Yaakov and Esther Schwob live with their eight children in Rehasim. Their eldest daughter, Yael, a teenager, was born with an enlarged red nose and a swollen upper lip. Doctors assured the worried new parents that these harmless birth defects would disappear in time. The doctors could not have been more wrong.

When Yael was only three months old, the massive and terrifying bleeding began. Yael's "birthmark" was actually a rare and potentially fatal birth defect called arterial-venus malformation (AVM). Simply put, the blood vessels at the site of the AVM, in this case, Yael's nose, are under abnormally high pressure, causing them to dilate, rupture and bleed uncontrollably. The location of the abnormal blood vessels in the center of Yael's face make her condition especially complex.

Yael has undergone eight operations in the hands of vascular surgeons in four countries and on three continents. Parts of her upper palate and upper lip have been removed, and although many efforts were made to save her decaying nose, it had to be amputated to stop life-threatening bleeding. And now, to complicate the situation further, the skin on Yael's nose area is deteriorating, so Yael cannot even wear her prosthetic nose. As a young woman, she feels embarrassed about her appearance. Yael refuses to attend school and now needs to be tutored at home. Hiring tutors to keep her up to speed with her school work is just another in the long list of expenses for this family.

And although the Schwobs face their problems with dignity and faith, the whole experience is difficult on them emotionally and financially. With the recent government cutbacks to the yeshivot in Israel, Yaakov's hours as a teacher in a yeshiva have been cut drastically. Esther, a kindergarten teacher, is unable to work full-time because she needs to be with Yael during her frequent and prolonged absences from school.

For a long time, the Schwobs were too proud to ask for or accept help. But, as Yael's situation deteriorated, they sorely needed an angel looking over them. So with Mark Pollack acting as an intermediary, Myriam and Lewis began sending sizeable donations to them every six months. For many months, the Schwobs didn't even know from whom the money was coming. "We didn't want them to feel indebted to us – we didn't want them to feel as if they had to thank us."

Myriam and Lewis are modest people, who did not want any publicity about their relationship with the Schwobs. However, the family's needs have become so great that the Gummermans are searching for others to help Yael in her struggle. "It looks as if Yael may be facing yet another operation," says Myriam. "The family is researching their options with a surgeon in North Carolina. And, even though the doctor has generously agreed to donate his services, the hospital bill will still probably run around $65,000 dollars." This is more than the Gummermans can handle on their own.

As Lewis and Myriam become more and more distressed over not being able to meet the Schwob's growing needs, they reached out to their friends for some financial support. They were sorely disappointed by the lack of response they received. That's when they decided to come out publicly so they could get more help for Yael and her family.

When the article about the Schwobs appeared in The Jewish Chronicle of Pittsburgh, people like Shelly Segal responded with an open heart and an open pocketbook. Following Shelly's lead, her young son Joseph got into the act. "He donated a portion of his bar mitzvah money to Yael's fund," says Myriam. "We wish that we could find more kids out there like Joseph who are willing to lend a hand. Would that be wonderful?" Indeed it would.

Myriam Gummerman traveled to Israel for her father's funeral. It was then that she spoke directly to Yaakov Schwob for the first time. He called to express his condolences. "When this all began, I didn't want to meet the Schwobs," recalls Myriam. "I wanted to keep this as anonymous as possible to save them from embarrassment. We never may meet face-to-face, but they and Yael are like part of the family. When I go shopping and I see something that Yael might like, I pick it up for her – just like I would do for one of my own children."

In an email to Myriam, Yaakov wrote; "As you know well by now, the only solution is in God's hands. May He who heals all beings, heal Yael completely. We thank God for giving us such a special person as Yael. She never complains and is always with a smile and a good word."

The Gummermans will continue to send money to the Schwobs as long as they can do so. It is their hope that other people will find the compassion to do so as well.

* Since this piece was written, Lewis Gummerman, ז"ל, passed away.

Stanlee J. Stahl

Repaying a Debt

The images in the video presentation produced by Stanlee Stahl for the Jewish Foundation for the Righteous captures the essence of her work. The film depicts Holocaust survivors surrounded by their children, grandchildren, and some with great-grandchildren – beautiful families, smiling for the camera. Then, by their sides, their rescuers – the righteous Gentiles – those people who stepped forward and faced unthinkably horrible consequences. Many times they risked their own safety in order to save a virtual stranger – just because it was the right thing to do. Those heroes probably never realized that in saving one person's life, they would be allowing an entire generation to flourish and grow.

How can one ever really repay almost superhuman acts of bravery and kindness? How can one thank another human being who risked his or her own life to rescue Jews during the Holocaust? Stanlee Stahl is a woman who is attempting to answer these questions.

Stanlee is the Executive Vice President of the Jewish Foundation for the Righteous, an organization that has two major functions: The first is to provide monthly financial assistance to more than 1,600 righteous Gentiles who put their own lives on the line to save Jews in thirty countries. "Most of these people are now frail and elderly and many are living in poverty, still in the countries where they performed their courageous acts," explains Stanlee. "At the annual dinner for the agency, I with an office staff of only four, raised more than 1.3 million dollars to parcel out to those rescuers in need. In many cases, the money is their only means of support." It is Stanlee's passion and zeal for their cause that convinces potential donors to give large sums of money.

"The Jewish Foundation for the Righteous (JFR) is in the business of fulfilling the *mitzvah* of *hakarat hatov*, searching and recognizing goodness," Stanlee says. "It is an interactive entity. I communicate with survivors and rescuers regularly. Yad Vashem (Israel's Holocaust Authority) might give them a medal or a diploma…and then will never have contact with them again. The JFR is the only link to these heroes and that part of our history."

The second function of the Foundation is to preserve the legacy of the rescuers through Holocaust education. The JFR engaged Professor Deborah Dwork, a leading Holocaust scholar, to write a book on the Holocaust. The book, *Voice and Views: A History of the Holocaust,* provides the adult learner/educator with a compilation of excerpts from landmark works in Holocaust scholarship. "Each of the ten chapters addresses an area that teachers need to understand before they can properly address this sensitive subject. For example, there is a section about 'anti-Judaism, Antisemitism' and another about 'Gentile life Under German Occupation.'" Stanlee explains, "I believe that it is difficult to appreciate the sacrifices and courage of the rescuers without knowing how difficult their lives were during that time period."

She attributes her involvement in *tikkun olam* to her late mother, Pearl. "My mother made me an O.R.T. orphan. When I was only eight years old, I was doing my own laundry, while my mother was off dedicating an O.R.T. school in Israel or some other remote destination," recalls Stanlee proudly. "My mother, who died several years ago, was the National Director of the American Magen David Adom for Israel (the support arm of Israel's Red Cross in the United States) and a major fundraiser. She led by example."

Summing up, Stanlee says, "When I meet the rescuers, I feel blessed. I sometimes wonder what I would do if confronted by similar situations. I hope that I would never have to find out. Jewish tradition has a great deal to offer me in terms of running this agency. It teaches me the value of human life and the rescuers are role models for how to make ethical and moral decisions. My job is a beautiful marriage between the Jewish and non-Jewish worlds."

Section 6

Lo Ta'amod al Dam Re'echa / Do Not Stand Idly by While the Blood of Your Neighbor is Being Shed

Nothing established by violence and maintained by force...can endure.
Blum, "For All Mankind"

Did you ever wonder what you would do if you saw someone else being hurt? Would you step in and try to offer your help? Would you confront a friend of yours if he or she was engaging in self-destructive behavior? It might be easier for you to decide if you know what Jewish tradition has to say. Jews have an obligation to protect others from violent or life-threatening situations.

This commandment is found in the Torah: "Do not stand idly by while the blood of your neighbor is shed" (Leviticus 19:16). The *Talmud* expounds on this *mitzvah*, "If one sees someone drowning, mauled by beasts or attacked by robbers one is obligated to save him...[although you are not required to do so if it risks your own life] and the pursued person must be saved even at the cost of the pursuer's life..." (BT, Sanhedrin 73a).

The Code of Jewish Law elaborates on this message, "He who hears heathens or informers plotting to harm a person is obliged to inform the intended victim. If he is able to appease the perpetrator and deter him from the act, but does not do so, he has violated the law 'Do not stand by while your neighbor's blood is shed'" (*Shulchan Aruch*, Ch.M. 426:1).

The Torah, therefore, prohibits us from being indifferent to the suffering of those around us. This tenet applies to myriad situations that arise in our culture, from getting help for victims of spousal and child abuse to assisting victims of violent crimes.

Some people still adhere to the stereotype that domestic violence does not exist within the Jewish community, which sometimes makes it more difficult for victims to seek and find appropriate assistance. Sadly, Jews are not immune to any of the ills that affect other segments of society. Many women who are not afraid to become involved spring into action when they see their neighbor in the way of physical or extreme emotional harm.

In this section, you will meet women who unselfishly give of themselves to help others in harm's way. You will read about women such as Linda Storfer who left her suburban home in New Jersey to save a baby from a Romanian orphanage.

Maxine Uttal

Finding a Place

For two years Maxine Uttal had been struggling successfully with her fight against drug addiction through participation in a 12-step program. After a long and painful battle, her life was falling into place. However, she felt removed from the Jewish community that she loved. "Twelve-step programs are indispensable in the rehabilitation process, but many Jews feel that these programs have Christian overtones," explains Maxine. "Then a friend told me about Jewish Alchoholics Chemically Dependent and Significant Others (JACS). I was never as excited about anything as I was to see the words Jewish and alcoholic in the same sentence. I believed that Jewish alcoholics were the rare exception to the rule, and I had never looked toward Jewish sources for support," says Maxine. "I decided to attend a JACS retreat in New York's Catskill Mountains. When I walked into the musty old hotel and spent a weekend with Jews recovering from the effects of alcohol and drug addiction, I felt as though the two most important parts of my life were coming together and allowed me to become integrated – truly an epiphany. We all believed that we were the exception, and then realized we weren't alone. I cried the entire weekend."

Maxine wrote an article about this first retreat, "Among the 200 participants were rabbis, *Chasidim* and people just like me. Our bond was a 12-step program and Judaism, and they were no longer mutually exclusive. I went to synagogue and prayed for those addicts who were not yet in recovery. I sat and talked until two in the morning with one of the bearded men about how to pray. I heard prayers recited in Hebrew that sounded to my ears like they were spoken directly to me by God. I sang songs I had never heard before that seemed like they were already written in my soul. I meditated with a rabbi and felt touched by angels. I learned that the religion of my ancestors was rich with substance that was meaningful to me. Even more, I gained faith that it really was God who carried me through the years of hell and who now blesses me with peace."

When Maxine returned to New York after the retreat, she was transformed into a committed volunteer. Then in 1996, Maxine became the Executive Director of JACS. Although this position is typically held by someone with a master's degree in Social Work, the search committee felt that through her volunteer activities Maxine had displayed the qualities necessary to run the agency.

"JACS does the work of *tikkun olam* (repairing the world) by bringing all of these Jews together who have a common need to be together outside of Judaism, while helping them see each other as Jewish sisters and brothers," she says. JACS saves lives. Addiction is a deadly disease because of denial. In the Jewish community denial is much stronger. We are raised to believe that we are too strong and too smart to become addicted. Neither one has anything to do with addiction. JACS provides a life preserver for Jews who are drowning and want to be saved.

As a result of her association with JACS, she feels part of Jewish life again. Maxine concluded, "I feel connected to anything Jewish. I love Jewish people. When I'm at a retreat, I feel like I'm in the bosom of my family." Although Maxine may not have the master's degree after her name, her love of Judaism and her understanding of addiction keep JACS growing and moving forward. Maxine says, "I rely on the collective wisdom of thousands who have gone before," a philosophy that clearly works for her and for the betterment of the Jews who suffer the horrors of chemical dependency.

Linda Storfer

From Romania – A Bundle of Love

There are moments in a woman's life that are so significant and meaningful that she cannot help but reflect back upon the events that brought her to that point. Each of us feels a particular pride when our child achieves the age of bar or bat mitzvah – but for Linda Storfer, this moment was even more intensely satisfying than for most of us. In a sense, her life with son David came full circle at his bar mitzvah. He became a Jewish adult – and she believes that it was a unique privilege to get him to that point.

About fourteen years ago, Linda and her husband, Bennett, of Teaneck, NJ, were watching television and saw an exposé about the children of Romanian orphanages. Anyone seeing that newscast would have been saddened by what they had seen – but most people would have shut off their television and gone back to their normal lives. Not so with Linda Storfer. Broken hearted after witnessing the horrific conditions in which these children were forced to exist, Linda somehow knew that she had to act.

Linda recalls, "people always want more than they have – that's just human nature. I already had two great kids – a boy and a girl. But I wanted more. And, by taking in this one child, I knew that I could make a difference in his life."

Logically, it would seem to make sense that if these deprived children were in such need, and someone was willing to adopt them, the process would be simple. But, in the situation of the Romanian orphans – logic did not prevail.

The Stofers hired a Romanian lawyer who promised to get them a baby and to make the process as easy as possible. "We were incredibly naïve," recalls Linda. "We believed everything that he told us." However, what they found when they arrived in Romania was a string of disappointments, horrible living conditions and worst of all – no baby. Bennett and Linda were moved from house to house. "There was no kosher food for us to eat," remembers Linda, "and the smell of Romanian sausage cooking made me feel physically ill."

The couple survived primarily on a diet of bread and water. And to make matters worse, they were separated from their two young children, Mandi and Matthew, during the Gulf War. They couldn't even call home to check on the children's safety or to find out what was going on in America or Israel. They were living in a total news and communications blackout in a backward, third-world country. Their lawyer seemed to be a skilled liar – making promise after promise that he never kept. Bennett and Linda were filled with guilt and anxiety about what was going on with their family back home. After two weeks, a frustrated Bennett returned to Teaneck – to the children and his business. But, a determined Linda stayed behind – frightened and alone.

During the next two weeks in Romania, Linda was moved again to yet another family. This time, however, the family provided some help. The hosts took Linda to a home where a young woman, abandoned by her husband, had given birth to a healthy baby boy. The new mother spoke to Linda through an interpreter. She didn't say much, other than she wanted her son to have a better life in a good home with a good family. Thus, out of a sense of love for her baby, she gave her child willingly to a family from across the world.

It was only at that moment when David, wrapped in rags, was handed to Linda, that she had the feeling that she was performing a *mitzvah*. "In that split second that I held David in my arms, I understood that I would have the privilege of raising this person as a Jewish child – and someday I would have the honor of seeing him become a bar mitzvah."

But Linda still had a long road ahead of her. She hired a baby nurse to care for David while she slogged through the paperwork in Romania. Finally, at the end of a long month, Linda left the country without her son. She had to get back to Matt and Mandi who needed her badly. Linda was plagued with guilt over missing nine-year-old Mandi's birthday party. And Linda's lawyer assured her that it was fine to leave and that David would be united with his new American family by the end of March of 1991.

When Linda returned home, she called the lawyer daily, but he didn't respond to her phone calls. March dragged on slowly, April came and went without David. There was an emptiness in Linda's heart and at her table on Pesach. Finally, she decided that unless she returned to Romania, she would never see David again. After spending an emotional Mother's Day with Bennett, Matt and Mandi, she was again boarded a plane for the arduous trip to Romania.

This time her lawyer actually met her at the airport. An exhausted Linda accompanied him straight to the courthouse where she signed all the necessary paperwork. This time, after only two days in Romania, an elated mother traveled back to New Jersey with David Jonathan Storfer. "He was the best behaved baby on the plane," Linda wistfully recalls. "He was so happy and full of smiles."

"I'm not a humanitarian," says Linda. "I just wanted to make one child's life better. What I did was not anything so special. He has enriched our lives and our other children's lives." In fact, little David had an entire family that doted on him. Two cribs were set up in the Storfer home – one in Matt's room and one in Mandi's. Two delighted older children took turns having David sleep by their bedsides.

Now at thirteen-years old, David is a happy kid. He loves his Jewish school, his friends and his life in Teaneck. "David is such an easy child. He's intelligent. He does well in school. He loves going to *shul* with us." On the day of his bar mitzvah, Linda and Bennett's life with David took on a special meaning. The moment had finally arrived that she had dreamed of from the time that David was first placed in her arms by his biological mother. She and Bennett had raised a Jewish child and he was about to enter Jewish manhood. The lives of the Storfer family are truly blessed.

Claire Ginsburg Goldstein

Bears From Bergenfield

Many of us have been emotionally distraught about the situation in Israel. Some of us have been touched in more personal ways by the terrorist attacks when people in our own families or communities have been murdered or maimed by homicide bombers. Many of us just don't know what to do to help. We feel frustrated, angry and sad.

Those were precisely the emotions that Claire Ginsburg Goldstein felt. Watching the news reports from Israel sickened her, but she was literally called into action several summers ago after she met an Israeli girl, Roni. One muggy day in August, there was a horrible terrorist attack in Israel. Roni, a beloved camp counselor of Claire's daughter, Shira, was hysterical when she heard the grisly news. She told Claire, "We feel so alone in Israel. Everyone is against us." Roni's sense of isolation touched Claire's heart and she felt she needed to do something to comfort the victims and let them know that American Jews cared a great deal about them.

Claire was not sure where to begin, but as she often does, she turned to her own children for inspiration. "I asked Sam and Shira how we could show the Israeli people that we care about them." After some thought and discussion, her then ten-year-old son, Sam, said, "How about sending Teddy Bears to kids in Israel who have been hurt?" Out of the mouths of babes. And that is how Bears from Bergenfield was born!

Since that time, Claire and her kids have sent approximately 22,000 bears and other stuffed animals to hospitals in Israel. This has been a real grassroots effort. The bears have come from all kinds of sources. Several people donated bears that they used for centerpieces for their bat or bar mitzvahs. Russ Berrie (a stuffed animal manufacturer) donated eleven dozen bears. Yeshiva and day school kids from Bergen County, NJ to Atlanta, GA raised money to purchase bears.

"I have met the most amazing people since I started this project, says Claire. "Meeting these kind and caring individuals has added so much to my life." She tells a story about Mrs. Friedman, a nursing home resident in Ridgewood, NJ. Mrs. Friedman lives in a non-Jewish home and is a friend of Claire's. Touched by the work that Claire was doing, Mrs. Friedman wanted to help. So, she placed some signs around the Home asking her fellow residents to donate bears. She placed a small box outside of her door to collect the animals. She was a little nervous that she might be disappointed by her friends' unwillingness to give, because after all, why would these elderly Gentile folks be interested in helping kids in Israel? However, over the next few weeks, Mrs. Friedman was inundated with bears until the total reached 500!

It seems that people do want to help, they just don't always know how. Claire's project is small enough in scope, yet large enough in meaning, that almost anyone can jump in and become involved. But how does she do it?

"When I started this project," recalls Claire, I barely knew how to turn on my computer, but since we founded Bears from Bergenfield, I've learned all sorts of tricks." Claire advertises on-line to find people to donate bears and to take duffle bags filled with them to Israel. She has met other people on-line (in Israel) who pick up the bears and then distribute them to hospitals. "Nobody who has promised to take bears to Israel and deliver them has ever not completed their job. It's amazing how this trust is immediate with total strangers."

Claire's biggest problem right now is finding enough volunteers who are willing to take a duffle bag or two filled with fifty-five bears with them to Israel. "We have never had a problem with security" she says. "I send the volunteers with a letter, and El Al is very helpful and cooperative." Through the help of a friend, Claire made a connection with the Aurora Teddy Bear Company in California. They have been nice enough to sell her beautiful Teddy Bears that retail for about twenty dollars for three dollars and fifty cents a piece.

"You cannot believe what this project has added to my life, enthuses Claire. "This project is like a quilt made up of many different people. Every person that I meet adds a piece to the quilt and adds to its beauty."

Section 7

Talmud Torah / The Study of Torah

He who possesses both learning and piety is like an artist with his tools ready to hand.
Yochanan b. Zakkai, *Avot de Rabbi Nathan*, 22

Those of you who don't like school may be surprised to discover that studying and learning are part of your heritage. Jews are often referred to as the "people of the book." Many attribute the endurance of the People of Israel to their emphasis on Torah study and the continual pursuit of wisdom; "Learning-learning-learning: that is the secret of Jewish survival" (Ahad HaAm).

In Jewish tradition, knowledge for its own sake is not enough; it must be a means to an end, which is the performance of *mitzvot*. In that sense, learning Torah serves a purpose: "Study is greater than practice because it leads to practice" (BT, Kiddushin 40b).

Jewish tradition dictates that the study of Torah is a lifelong calling; "The road to learning is endless" (Jacob ben Asher, Tokheha, 14c). In addition, we are commanded to pass on Torah learning to our offspring; "You shall teach them diligently to your children" (Deuteronomy 6:7).

There are many Jewish women who are exceptionally gifted educators, serious about their own studies and successful in their desire to bring others closer to Torah. Their work exemplifies the premise: "The world stands on three things: on Torah, prayer, and deeds of loving-kindness" (Pirkei Avot 1:2).

Some women, like Judith Helfand, teach Torah values in unusual ways. Judith uses the medium of film to teach her audience about Judaism and our respect for the environment and for human life.

Sarah Labkowski

An Oxymoron: A Chassidic Feminist...Or is it?

The Jewish section of Crown Heights in Brooklyn, NY resembles Russian villages that existed a hundred years ago. It is an eclectic neighborhood where African-Americans and Chassidic Jews live side by side. Dotting this concrete *shtetl* (a neighborhood akin to a small village in Eastern Europe) are signs that herald the coming of the *Moshiach* (the Messiah), others that anticipate the arrival of *Shabbat*, and still others that advise us that Israel is a gift from *Hashem* (God). Many families have larger than life-sized photographs of the beloved, Lubavitcher Rebbe (their late chief Rabbi), Menachem Mendel Schneerson, *zt"l*, hanging on the front of their homes. There are numerous Judaica shops and many others that peddle clothing and furniture for children. Lubavitcher Chassidim generally have large families, and many women can be seen wheeling double, and triple, strollers. Men sport black suits, black hats, white shirts and long beards, and the women cover their hair and wear long skirts and blouses that cover their elbows and collarbones, despite the uncomfortably high temperature and humidity in Brooklyn.

Sarah Labkowski is a legend in Crown Heights. She is the founder and administrator of Machon Chana, a woman's *yeshiva* (school of intensive Jewish learning). Sarah says, "I have a singular focus, to educate and empower Jewish women," When Sarah speaks, she never looks at her watch or breaks eye-contact, or accepts telephone calls (unless it is from one of her twelve children). She makes each person with whom she interacts feel as if they have her undivided attention for however long they need it. According to her students, making each young woman believe that she is special is one of Sarah's greatest talents.

Sarah recalls her thoughts as a serious little girl, "The role of Jewish women in Lubavitch life bothered me. I was unsure if I would be able to find my niche within my own community. I'm a Lubavitch feminist, if that's possible, and I needed to understand my mission on earth. I voiced my concerns to my father, telling him that I needed to learn in order to find meaning in my life. Instead of becoming angry with me for questioning his beliefs, my father encouraged me to take an intellectual approach to *Chassidism*. We started a tradition of engaging in a weekly *shiur* (a session where she and her father could study Jewish texts together), a practice we continue to this day. My father whet my appetite for spirituality and Jewish learning, and I soon realized that I was meant to educate other Jewish women."

She began to teach classes on *chassidic* philosophy, accompanied by cake and coffee in her living room, which were tremendously popular and attracted increasingly larger groups of students. Thrilled with the overwhelmingly positive response, Sarah felt she was quickly outgrowing the confines of her home and dreamed of establishing a *yeshiva*. As is customary in her community, she approached the Rebbe for his permission. The Lubavitcher Rebbe gave her plan his blessing in a letter. He wrote, "Such a school for women is of great responsibility...and perhaps is even more important than a similar school for men." Sarah explains, "The Rebbe had a vision of educating the entire world to see the beauty of Judaism. He felt the key to Jewish continuity was through women, and allowed the institution to be named Machon Chana, in memory of his beloved mother, Rebbetzin Chana, *zt"l*."

With the support of her Rebbe, Sarah Labkowski began her journey. Machon Chana grew from a fledgling school that educated only a few women into an institution that now occupies a large building plus two dormitories, and which boasts thousands of alumnae worldwide. There are about seventy full time students and fifty part-timers at the *yeshiva*. Woman come from places as far flung as Zimbabwe, Peru, Israel, Australia and Germany. Typically, at any given time, half the students are from outside the United States, giving instructors the added challenge of teaching women who may not speak English about Judaism and the *Chassidic* lifestyle. Sarah helps each young woman find her own place in the community by asking questions and continually seeking answers.

Judith Helfand

A Healthy Baby Girl

Judith Helfand frequently speaks to groups of teenagers about environmental issues and their impact on the lives of ordinary people. "I ask them if they can pinpoint the first time they were outraged as a result of an injustice that was perpetrated upon someone else. Could they think back and remember when they first felt empathy for an occurrence so unfair and so egregious that they couldn't walk away from it? I can recall with great clarity when that exact moment happened for me." Judith, at fourteen and recovering at home from a broken leg and trying to stave off boredom, she turned on the "Phil Donahue Show," and listened as a young woman told how her mother had taken the drug diethylstilbestrol (DES) during pregnancy to try to avoid a miscarriage. As a result, the daughter developed a rare form of vaginal cancer and needed to have a hysterectomy. Judith remembers her anger and disgust as she learned that even though animal studies had shown that DES was carcinogenic, and even though it was found to be useless in preventing miscarriages, drug companies, concerned only with their profits, callously continued to promote its use.

"When my mother walked in the door from work, I hit her with a barrage of emotions about what I had just seen and heard. My mother seemed to be listening, but she was strangely, almost eerily, silent. I looked up and saw that my mother had turned ghastly pale, totally devoid of color," Judith recounts. "The irony of the situation was surreal, but somehow just by looking at my mother's face – I knew. My mother had wanted to tell me as soon as I got my first period, but she didn't want to spoil the moment. In the months that followed, she wanted to tell me, but then it was my bat mitzvah and she didn't want to ruin the occasion." When was a good time to deliver that brand of news? Suddenly, there was no choice. In the shelter of their Long Island home, Judith's mother reluctantly conceded that she, too, along with tens of thousands of unsuspecting women, had taken DES during pregnancy.

Judith was shocked to learn that she was a "victim" of a phenomenon which was only beginning to be understood. How could her life change that drastically from one minute to the next? Judith knew one thing from the outset. Although she was terrified, she was not going to keep silent. "I wanted to scream about this outrage from the roof tops so that everyone would know about the horror that had now unceremoniously become a part of my life."

For the next several years, Judith had an annual checkup to determine whether she would become a casualty of this insidious form of cancer, which typically afflicted women in their late teens and early 20s. The terror was always lurking. Each time she was granted a reprieve and pronounced healthy. By the time she turned twenty and did not have cancer, the prevailing wisdom was that she was "home free" – she had dodged the bullet.

Yet, her own good fortune didn't stop her from wanting to make a difference in the world. On graduating from the New York University Film School, she decided to pursue a career in documentary film making, working on projects that would promote social change. Making movies would be her way of becoming an activist.

At twenty-three, Judith was young and healthy; her world was a boundless menu of possibilities. Nevertheless, she volunteered to assist on a film that was being made about DES babies. It had been three years since her last trip to the doctor, but while working on this project, she learned of cases of cancer diagnosed in women in their late twenties and early thirties. She was stunned. Again her world was shaken – she wasn't as safe as she had thought. The film-makers insisted she schedule a checkup, and this time the news was bad. Judith had cancer. Judith said, "The first thing I thought of when I was told was 'what is this going to do to my mother?' The second thing was, 'I'm not going to be able to have children. What would my bubbe have said?'" Two weeks after this discovery, she had a radical hysterectomy, during which her uterus, Fallopian tubes and the top third of her vagina were removed. She would never bear children, and would always live with the threat of recurrence. Judith recalls, "I remember waking up after that surgery and feeling as if something had been taken from me." All of this loss and suffering afflicted Judith because her mother, like any woman after two miscarriages, wished to have a healthy baby and trusted that DES would be the answer to her prayers.

Judith's personal saga immediately became the film's focus. The crew was with her during the initial diagnosis and accompanied her home from the hospital. She viewed making the movie as a way to help herself and her family heal. "However, in short order, it became clear to me that the film makers did not have the funds or wherewithal to produce the kind of documentary I believed needed to be made," Judith explains. "I took over, borrowing a video camera from my cousin and setting it up in the corner of my bedroom. I needed to tell my own story from the inside out." What resulted from her five-year endeavor was a chronicle of the pain, misery, guilt and healing that she and her parents endured. *"A Healthy Baby Girl"* won a prestigious Peabody Award and was shown at Robert Redford's Sundance Film Festival.

"A Healthy Baby Girl" has become Judith's way of shouting about DES from the roof tops. She has transformed her experience into a vehicle to teach others what environmental toxins can do to a human body and to a person's life. The film is a jumping-off point to educate groups about the dangers of toxic chemicals such as the plague of dioxins (chemical cousins of DES) which are emitted into the air when hospitals incinerate hazardous waste. Judith's portrayal of her and her family's struggle has inspired many to advocate for a safer environment. She particularly focuses her speaking on

Jewish groups because she feels that the "best activism starts at home. You can't ask other people to do what your own community doesn't do. I view my involvement with the Jewish world as an extension of telling my own story from the inside out. Jewish women are an incredibly smart, powerful population. As Jews, we are committed to caring for our families and if you care for your family, then you have to care about the environment." Judith talks about what the Hebrew expression *L'dor V'dor* (from one generation to another) means to her, "I understand the concept of passing Judaism down from one generation to another inside the home. We pass down holidays, celebrations and rituals. But then, we have to go outside of the family and into the world and pass down a sense of ethics and justice. If we see something that is broken, we have to make an attempt to fix it – that's *tikkun olam* – repairing the world."

Klezmer music flows through Judith's film. To her, these lilting, poignant melodies, uniquely Jewish and Eastern European, are representative of her sense of continuity. Klezmer music has been passed down from one generation to another and is frequently played at weddings and bar mitzvahs. "I believe that it was the heedlessness and irresponsibility of the chemical companies that took away my chances of handing my own tradition and culture to my children. This opportunity has been violently and permanently ripped away. I hope that perhaps this music, which is associated with families and happy times, will make chemical companies understand that an acceptable level of risk encompasses real families, real people, with real feelings."

Marla Berkowitz

The Light she Emits

Watching Naomi Brunn interpret the weekly Torah portion is mesmerizing. Her hands move so quickly and with such intensity that they resemble birds playing a game of tag in the sky, and her facial expressions and body language are purely theatrical. How can she so quickly translate the complex liturgical and Biblical Hebrew into American Sign Language? And for whom is she interpreting with such feeling? Naomi, an American Sign Language interpreter provides the channel through which Marla Berkowitz, the first Deaf Wexner Fellow and the first Deaf student to attend the Davidson School of the Jewish Theological Seminary (J.T.S.), can finally derive meaning from attending synagogue services.

"I was raised in a Conservative household where the rhythm of the family's life revolved around *Shabbat* dinner with family and friends and celebrating Jewish holidays and lifecycle events. I am the only Deaf member of my family, and attended synagogue regularly with them, but I had no access to the experience and felt isolated and bored," says Marla. "I was attracted to and connected with anything Jewish, but there was no avenue available to me to pray with other Jews. I curiously watched people returning weekly to *Shabbat* services, and wondered why they bothered to sit though something so deadly. Almost instinctively, I knew that there must be something to it, and hoped that someday I would be part of a synagogue that would have something spiritual to offer me."

In 1993, Marla was employed as a case worker at the New York Society for the Deaf where she counseled Deaf, HIV-positive clients. The experience of working day in and day out with individuals facing their own mortality brought up many theological questions. It was painful to deal with these life and death issues without the support of organized Jewish life. But since doors were closed to Marla, those questions went unanswered.

Then by luck or coincidence, or maybe it was *beshert*, the agency hired Naomi Brunn, an A.S.L. interpreter, who is a product of a Hebrew day school, and holds a bachelor's degree with a minor in Hebrew. Naomi was exuberant and full of ideas to enrich the lives of the Deaf. One day she approached Marla and asked if she had any interest in teaming up and making synagogue life in New York City accessible to Deaf Jews – a match made in heaven.

Thus, the duo founded an organization called Manhattan Young Adult Jewish Deaf, utilizing the acronym MiYAD which, in Hebrew, means "immediately." They chose that particular word because the Deaf are always told to "wait" for entrance into different aspects of society, and they wanted to accomplish this particular feat "now."

Marla and Naomi began discussing their concerns for Deaf Jews with rabbis all over the city. They met with a great deal of resistance and disinterest. "Many times during this process, we felt exhausted, angry and marginalized," recalls Marla. "But we refused to give up. Then luckily we landed at the doorstep of Congregation B'nai Jeshuren (B.J.) and talked with Rabbi Roly Matalon and Rabbi Marcel Bronstein." Both men listened carefully, and immediately agreed to assist Marla in getting anything she required to make B.J. approachable to Deaf Jews. Marla was stunned by their positive response. "I wasn't sure they really comprehended what actually was entailed in making this dream into a reality. At first I believed they might be paying lip service to the concept," remembers Marla. "What I didn't appreciate, at that point, is that their desire to include all Jews in their community is so imbedded in their thinking that making B.J. a place where Deaf Jews could participate came naturally."

Marla hired Naomi to work as the interpreter for many functions at B'nai Jeshuren. When one translates from another language into A.S.L., the method employed is "meaning-based" rather than word-for-word. Since Naomi is knowledgeable in Hebrew and understands the structure of the liturgy and the nuances of the language, she brings much more to her interpretation than most other people could. In this circumstance, the interpreter filters much of the input, and has to be tremendously skilled so that the message and feeling of the prayers and Torah readings are not lost.

Marla explained, "Now that I had established that connection with Jewish life in a more formal way, nothing was going to stop me from increasing my Jewish learning and involvement. Marla now attends J.T.S. through the generosity of a Wexner grant and is doing pioneering research in the field of Jewish Deaf education. It took six months of negotiating with J.T.S. for Marla to obtain the services she needed to function in this environment, including skilled interpreters and note takers, but now she has a workable system in place.

Aside from work on her master's degree and her continuing involvement with B.J., Marla, together with Naomi, founded another organization called The Jewish Deaf Resource Center, Inc. She describes this association as parallel to the New York Society for the Jewish Blind, serving as a clearinghouse for resources to make the greater Jewish community aware of how to make services accessible to the Deaf, how to nurture Jews who are Deaf to become Jewish professionals, and how to train interpreters in liturgy and Jewish texts. The organization recently received its first grant from the Nathan Cummings Foundation and Ruth Durshlag, and hired a rabbi and an A.S.L. interpreter to develop a curriculum to train interpreters to work within the Jewish community.

"I plan to spend five months in Israel studying the resources available for Deaf Jews there," says Marla. "When I return and finish my degree I hope that I will ultimately work for The Jewish Deaf Resource Center, providing support for Deaf Jews and their families. I have a dream that someday I will found a Jewish Day School for the Deaf, similar to institutions that existed in Europe prior to World War II. At this juncture, parents are faced with the painful reality that day schools and *yeshivot* in America are not accessible to Deaf children."

Marla summed up her accomplishments over the past few years in this way, "I had a thirst for spirituality.… Naomi has given me a chance to nurture that spark…she opened the door…and allowed the spark to be lit." Due to her own persistence, the help of a talented interpreter and devoted friend, and the sensitivity of two rabbis, Marla has been able to share her talents and inspiration with a very fortunate Jewish community.

* Marla is now the President of the Jewish Deaf Congress.
** Naomi is now Naomi Brunnlehrman and is the first interpreter in the country to have an MA degree in order to specialize in Jewish A.S.L., interpreting without having to rely on "interpreting notes."

Section 8

Kavod Hamayt, Nichum Avaylim /
Honoring the Dead and Comforting the Bereaved

It is better to go to a house of mourning, than to a house of feasting.
Ecclesiastes, 7:2

Honoring the dead is a *mitzvah* you probably haven't heard much about. Even if you have experienced a death in your family, you probably don't know all of the laws and customs pertaining to death. However, you may have already come to appreciate how Jewish communities rally around the bereaved offering comfort and support.

Typically, women who perform *mitzvot* pertaining to the dead or mourning, do them quietly, out of respect for the dignity and privacy of those involved. Honoring the dead is the ultimate form of *chesed*, termed *chesed shel emet* (a true act of loving-kindness) because it is a deed that can never be repaid by the recipient. Jewish law and custom dictates a host of appropriate behaviors associated with death and dying. "A dying person should not be left alone because he should not feel abandoned in his last moments, and also because of the sobering effect death has on the living" (Shulchan Aruch, Y.D. 339:4). Jewish tradition teaches us that the body houses the soul, and is entitled to respect even after the spirit has departed from it. Therefore, a corpse should not be left alone. Before the funeral, the *tahara* (ritual washing and purification) of the body is done in the funeral home, usually by members of the *Chevra Kaddisha* (burial society). Only Jewish women ritually prepare other Jewish women for burial.

There is no obligatory service for a Jewish funeral. Typically, the *Kaddish* (prayer for the dead) and various psalms are recited. It is customary for a rabbi, a close friend or a family member to deliver a eulogy. A simple pine, closed coffin is most desirable. "The deceased once were buried in ornate caskets, and the poor in cheap coffins; so the rabbis have decreed that all who die, however rich or poor, be buried in plain caskets" (BT, Mo'ed Katan 27a).

Burying the dead is an act of loving-kindness and can be traced back to the Torah. The subject of burial is first mentioned in the book of Genesis (Gen. 23:4), when Abraham buries his wife, Sarah: "I am a stranger and sojourner with you; give me a possession of a burying place with you, that I may bury my dead out of sight." According to the Biblical commentator, Rashi, "...the reverential concern which the Patriarch shows to give honorable burial to his dead has been a distinguishing feature among his descendants. Care of the unburied body of a friendless person, takes precedence over all other commandments."

After the funeral, Jews have a responsibility to comfort the mourners when the *shiva* (seven-day period of mourning) begins. People visit the bereaved to express their condolences and come together to form a *minyan* (a quorum of ten Jewish adults necessary to recite specific prayers) allowing the family to recite the Mourner's *Kaddish* (the prayer for the dead). Many kids and often some adults feel uncomfortable in a *shiva* house, unable to think of something appropriate to say. Adhering to Jewish custom makes this situation a little easier. Visitors are not supposed to speak to the mourners unless they initiate conversation. It is most appropriate to sit quietly with the bereaved and allow them to take the lead. A simple "I'm sorry" and a warm hug can never be wrong.

According to the *Shulchan Aruch* (Code of Jewish Law), "On the first day of mourning, the mourner is forbidden to eat his own food at the first meal. It is, therefore, the duty of neighbors to send a "meal of condolence." The mourners should begin with eggs or lentils, which are round and have no mouth (dent), just as the mourner presumably has no mouth" (*Shulchan Aruch*, 205:2).

There are many activities that fulfill the *mitzvah* of *kavod hamayt* and *nichum avaylim*. In some cities in the United States, individuals are paid to guard, ritually wash, and bury the corpse. However, in many Jewish communities there is a trend toward returning those responsibilities to the hands of family members and friends. Women are involved in helping people cope with death by making it a more personal, and thereby a more meaningful, experience. In many cases, the bereaved feel comforted by performing these rituals themselves or by knowing that they are being accomplished by someone within their own community as an act of *chesed shel emet*.

Rena Halpern Kieval

God is Closest to Those with Broken Hearts

Beruriah, the wife of Rabbi Meir and a Talmudic scholar in her own right, was immortalized in a poignant *Midrash* which demonstrates her compassionate nature. In the midst of her own horrific pain over the loss of her two sons, she searches for a way to cushion the devastating blow for her husband. Beruriah says to him:

> *"Some time ago I was entrusted by a friend with some jewels for safekeeping and now he wants them back. Shall I return them?"*

> *"Of course," answered Rabbi Meir, "the jewels must be returned."*

> *Beruriah then took him to where their dead sons were lying. When he collapsed and cried, she gently reminded him;*

> *"Did you not say we must return to the owner the precious jewels he entrusted to us? The Lord has given and the Lord has taken away. Blessed be the name of the Lord."*

Rena Halpern Kieval is forty-something, with a husband, Shalom, and two sons, David and Daniel, attempting to transform one of life's most devastating experiences into something positive. Like Beruriah, she has emerged from her own suffering by caring for others.

Rena and Shalom were a flawless match. He attended Columbia University, followed by Harvard Medical School. She graduated from Barnard College, then Boston University School of Social Work. Two superstars, they were bright, attractive, well-educated children of respected Conservative Rabbis. They met, courted, and married, and both families were thrilled. Everything moved along according to plan, and Rena, by then a social worker, began her career helping families in crisis.

A few years later, she gave birth to David, a perfect, beautiful son. Three years passed, and Rena delivered another son, Jonathan, also beautiful, but far from perfect. Through some twist of fate, the couple had a genetic predisposition to produce children with a particularly devastating group of symptoms, a syndrome uniquely their own.

Following a normal and uneventful pregnancy, Jonathan Gabriel Kieval was born with hydrocephalus (an enlarged head caused by an accumulation of fluid) and suffered from a host of complicated physical and neurological disorders. "I was shocked that something so awful could happen to my baby. In one moment my role in life changed from an average, working mother, to that of the caretaker of a severely disabled child. The months following his arrival were horrendously difficult. Many times Jonathan came close to death. He underwent numerous, life-threatening operations, and each time his chances seemed slim. Yet somehow, he pulled through." Rena worried constantly about his survival and about inflicting pain on an innocent baby.

When Rena and Shalom finally brought him home, they still needed to supplement his breathing with oxygen. He required frequent trips to the emergency room for treatment of one crisis after another. Rena explained, "I was thrown into a new world that revolved around specialists: occupational, physical and speech therapists, neurologists and developmental pediatricians. It was a whirlwind, attending to the needs of a growing preschooler and a special needs infant." In the midst of her own turmoil, she still found time to hire a babysitter on a weekly basis, not to go to the gym or get a haircut, but to counsel parents of children in the Neonatal Intensive Care Unit of a Boston hospital. She was establishing a lifelong pattern of dealing with stress and pain by helping others.

By the time Jon was four years old, his acute medical concerns were resolved and he was seemingly a healthy young boy. He had an engaging smile and a twinkle in his eye. Exceedingly articulate and animated, Jon memorized the make and model of everyone's automobile and sang his favorite songs in a clear, sweet voice. He loved to eat at Friendly's and adored the music of James Taylor. He had a gift for saying the things one often wants to say, but can't, because of social conventions. Once when he received a birthday present that he obviously didn't particularly like, he said with a friendly smile, "Thanks anyway."

During this time another son, Daniel, was born, but caring for Jon was still a major focus for despite his myriad abilities he was paradoxically unable to perform some of the simplest tasks. Jon was habitually overwhelmed by his environment, often looking lost and out of place. He slept little and became agitated easily. His capacity to exercise judgment or make decisions was restricted. Although he was fascinated by words and letters, his ability to comprehend what he read was limited. There was little hope that he would ever live an independent life.

For ten years, Rena devoted herself, day and night, to the care of Jonathan Gabriel and her other two boys. She spent much of her "free" time volunteering at the Hebrew Day School where David was enrolled, the special needs school that Jonathan attended, and the synagogue. She instituted a program at the synagogue, called *Nitzanim*, for preschool children and their parents during *Shabbat* morning services. At the Hebrew Day School she used her expertise in Hebrew language to teach adult education classes.

Just a few months after his tenth birthday, Rena and Shalom awoke one morning to find Jonathan, dead. He had gone to sleep the previous night, with a mild stomach bug, a typical childhood illness. Shalom recalls that Jon felt "almost weightless" when he carried him to bed that evening. The cause of Jon's death still remains a mystery.

The months that followed took on a nightmarish quality for the family as they endured and suffered through their shock and grief. Each day, Rena struggled to get out of bed and attend to the needs of her surviving boys. But get up she did. She took one difficult, painful gulp of air after the next and put one weighty foot in front of the other. Her suffering and anguish were palpable.

Gradually and quietly, Rena began to accomplish incredible things. She had always performed *mitzvot*, but they were taking a new direction because of what she was living through. She channeled the love and the longing she felt for Jon into doing work with others who also were bereaved. First, she helped people she knew, sitting for long hours with a friend's daughter while her mother lay dying in a hospice, running to *minyan* anytime someone needed to recite *kaddish,* and teaching a course to medical students on how to treat parents of disabled children with sensitivity. Performing acts of *chesed* for others was slowly bringing her back to life.

One day she announced that she had plans to create an organization named *Yad Yonatan* (Jonathan's Hand), the purpose of which was to fulfill the needs of the members of her large synagogue in times of loss. She designed a plan where each family would receive the services they required at their most difficult moments. Some would need a person to stay in their home during the funeral; others might require a babysitter for young children; still others might want someone to prepare, arrange, and serve food during the *shiva*. In accordance with Jewish custom, volunteers are assigned to sit with the deceased from the time of death until the funeral. A women's *Chevra Kadisha*, which lovingly prepares the body for burial, is now also part of the committee's activities. Someone from *Yad Yonatan* would organize nightly and morning *minyanim* at the house of mourning. The list of potential needs and organizational skills necessary to fill was endless, but Rena was undaunted.

In the years since *Yad Yonatan* was established, Rena has enlisted scores of people to assist her, and it is hard to imagine how the synagogue functioned before its existence. When someone passes away, Rena and her crew spring into action like a troupe of angels, filling in wherever and however needed in a dignified and unassuming manner. They have all been trained by Rena to offer comfort in a self-effacing and gentle manner.

Partly as a result of these life-transforming experiences, Rena became increasingly committed to serving the Jewish people and bringing them closer to the richness of Jewish tradition. She began to fulfill several rabbinic roles at her synagogue, and trained as a chaplain at a major medical center in upstate New York, where she works part-time as the Jewish spiritual care representative visiting and counseling Jewish patients and their families. Most recently, she decided to become a rabbi and was ordained, after commuting between her home in upstate New York to New York City to attend classes, at the Academy for Jewish Religion, an independent seminary that trains rabbis and cantors to serve Jews from all denominations.

Rena is a unique woman whose life exemplifies *chesed* and who continues to develop that life, even in the face of great personal pain. Like Beruriah, she puts the feelings of others above her own and shows infinite compassion and grace in the midst of unimaginable grief.

Leatrice Rabinsky

Journeys of Conscience

Trudging through the remains of Eastern Europe's concentration camps with a group of high school students is a grueling experience physically and emotionally. It is difficult to answer children's unanswerable questions and to watch innocents come face-to-face with some of the worst atrocities that human beings have ever perpetrated upon other human beings. Why did Leatrice Rabinsky begin making these "journeys of conscience" over thirty years ago and why does she, now in her seventies, continue to lead these trips?

"The theme of the Holocaust has been central to my life since I was a young girl," explains Leatrice. "In 1947, a close friend of ours brought nine Holocaust survivors, remnants of an extended family, from Europe. These people, particularly Ruthie and Sylvia, who were the same ages as my sister and I, 15 and 17, had a huge and formative influence on me. When the two girls arrived, they could speak only Hungarian, and yet the friendship between the four of us blossomed. I felt shock and some guilt because while my sister and I could study at high school, have fun and participate in after school activities, Ruthie and Sylvia had to work in a necktie factory to help support their family and learn English at night. After five or six months, when they could finally communicate in English, Ruthie tearfully confided in me about the horrible way that their mother had perished at Auschwitz. This devoted woman had given her own food to her daughters until she ultimately starved herself to death. Ruthie and Sylvia sat helplessly by as their mother died before their eyes. I have maintained friendships with these women and many other survivors. It was only last spring when Ruthie confided me about how sad she feels at no longer being able to remember her mother's face. This is one of the ramifications of the Holocaust." It was through her experiences and associations with people like Ruthie and Sylvia that Leatrice developed her overwhelming desire to keep alive the memory of those who were murdered, sustain the emotional lives of those who survived, and to spread the message of tolerance.

In 1965, Leatrice began teaching at Wiley Junior High School. She says, "I decided to undertake a two-week unit on Holocaust studies, which was in those days a novel idea in a public school setting. I invited speakers, who were survivors, to address my class. Five years later, I transferred to Cleveland Heights High School, where a creative administrator encouraged teachers to develop curricula based on their own interests, promising that, if there were enough "takers" for a class, then it would be would be included in the school's offerings. So I developed a course in Holocaust Literature which attracted two sections, each filled with thirty students."

"After teaching about the Holocaust for awhile, I decided that what the students needed to really understand the magnitude of this period in history was a journey to see what they were studying," recalls Leatrice. "Thirty years ago the idea of visiting the concentration camps was not well-accepted, and many thought I was crazy. But in October of 1975, I brought a request before the Cleveland Jewish Federation to fund "A Journey of Conscience," and miraculously, on December 17, only two months later, we departed for frigid and uninviting Poland. The Ratner, Miller Shafran Foundation supported our venture."

Leatrice's friend and Holocaust survivor, Bertha Lautman, who had promised herself that one day she would walk through the gates of Auschwitz as a free woman, joined her on this mission. Subsequently, Leatrice and Gertrude Mann, close friend, Cleveland Heights High student teacher and mission participant, wrote a book entitled *Journey of Conscience: Young People Respond to the Holocaust*, based on the experiences of this first group.

On each subsequent trip the students would return and culminate their experience by creating a "Journal of Testimony," a collection of essays and poetry detailing their experiences in Europe. In addition, Leatrice helped the students to create programs to combat hatred and bigotry.

Many of the students, some of whom are now in their late thirties or early forties, have become leaders within their own Jewish and non-Jewish communities. This experience in high school changed the course of many of their lives. One such individual is Rabbi Gary Robuck, formerly the spiritual leader of *Shar'ei Tikvah*, a Conservative congregation in Cleveland, now a rabbi in Sydney, Australia. Rabbi Robuck, has developed a program called "Face-to-Face" or in Hebrew, *"Panim-el-Panim,"* where public school students come to his synagogue, eat lunch, learn about basic Judaism and the Holocaust. This past year, 2,000 children took advantage of this hugely successful endeavor. Thus, Leatrice's work has had a ripple effect that includes Cleveland and each of the places her alumni live.

So what did Leatrice do to permanently affect and alter the lives of so many? She is a role model for social activism and facilitates creativity in her students inspiring them to become leaders. In an article written several years ago in the Cleveland Heights newspaper about her impending retirement, Leatrice explained, "There is life beyond the walls of the school. I don't just teach a subject, I teach human beings." Her students leave her care feeling empowered – believing that they can change the course of history.

Ronnie Shonzeit

Voices for Israel

On the night of the infamous Sbarro Pizza bombing in Israel, music producer and vocalist, Jordan Gorfinkel felt too distraught to make music at the *simcha* at which he was performing. But, the rabbi there advised him that "he must sing...otherwise the terrorists would win." That night Jordan sang his heart out, but still felt powerless to lend a hand to his brethren in Israel.

Through conversations with other musician friends, Jordan tried to find a meaningful way to comfort the victims of terror through music. After a great deal of discussion, they developed the idea of producing a CD using many different artists. Jordan wanted to create something that would support terror victims in the same way that Michael Jackson's, famed "We are the World" CD aided famine victims. Thus, "Voices for Israel" was born.

The seed for this inspiration was planted, but Ronnie Shonzeit entered the scene just in time to help the project blossom. "Our home has an open door policy," recalls Ronnie. "Jordan was staying at our apartment in Manhattan in order to pitch the idea to us. He was concerned about how he was going to attract 'big names' to donate their time to the project. He felt that with my organizational skills, I could make a significant contribution. And, the idea was so appealing and Jordan's enthusiasm was so contagious, that I just got on the phone. I called Dudu Fisher and he said 'sure.'" Ronnie quickly assumed her place at "Voices for Israel" as the volunteer assistant producer.

Jordan drafted Yehuda!, the internationally renowned Jewish music recording artist to serve as the musical director. Yehuda! oversaw the vocal and musical arrangements as well as the overall technical production. All of this activity took place in Ronnie's Upper West Side apartment. Ronnie kept long hours, talking to artist's agents and convincing them that this was a worthwhile endeavor. Though she had no previous experience in the entertainment industry, Ronnie learned by trial and error. Through a great deal of perseverance, and an extremely convincing nature, she was able to attract some of the biggest names in Jewish music. Once production began, Ronnie was busy feeding the artists, maintaining their schedules and, in order to save money, turning her home into a makeshift recording studio. "Basically, I acted as a Jewish mother. I did what I could to keep everyone happy," remembers Ronnie. "It was an amazing process to watch and I was privileged to be part of it."

Ronnie's four children; Gabriel, Jeremy, Yael and Jacob, were awed by the production as well. They were starry-eyed when they returned from school to find groups like Blue Fringe or The Chevra sitting around in their living room. The children performed the *mitzvah* of *hachnasat orchim* on many occasions, by serving food and giving up their own beds to help out with the project. When "Voices for Israel" was officially established as a non-profit organization it became even more of a family affair when Ronnie's husband, Andrew (along with Ronnie, of course), became one of the first board members.

The result? Fifty-four of the best known artists in Jewish music from across a wide religious and political spectrum banded together to produce a magnificent 2-CD set boasting thirty-six songs and a stirringly beautiful five minute video. "Voices for Israel" features the music of solidarity, hope, unity and peace. The performers have all donated their time.

Ronnie recommends the following, "buy the CD, slip it into your computer and listen to the title track while watching the video. Anyone with a Jewish soul will be moved by what they see and hear. Just listening to the theme song, '*Chazak Amenu*: We Stand As One' reminds us all of why we love Israel and why we must support her in these turbulent times. Proceeds from the sales of this CD are being turned over to already existing agencies in Israel that provide aid to terror victims.

One of the highlights of the CD is *Shir Lismo'ach* (Malki's Song), written by fifteen-year-old Malki Roth, just months before she was murdered in the Sbarro restaurant terrorist bombing. The song was recorded specifically for "Voices for Israel" by American star Yehuda!, who is joined by Yishai Lapidot, the leader of Oif Simchas, Malki's favorite band in Israel.

And what does Ronnie do now that the CD has been successfully launched? Call her cell phone and you'll hear the following message, "this is Ronnie Shonzeit and "Voices for Israel." Promoting this CD – getting the word out – has become Ronnie's mission as executive director. Spending her days answering emails from all parts of the globe, sending out press releases and arranging publicity events has become Ronnie's *reason d'etre*. "Just today," says Ronnie, "I heard from a woman in Calgary who wanted to buy fifty CDs. I've gotten emails from people in Australia. Everyone loves the CD once they hear it. It's amazing."

Ronnie's hard work is paying off. Jordan was recently a guest on "JM in the AM" (Jewish music in the morning – a radio show). "Host Nachum Segal is a big fan of 'Voices for Israel' and he's been really supportive," enthused Ronnie. Jordan will also appear on Zev Brenner, and Five Towns Radio has been playing the CDs. Jewish newspapers all of the world are writing articles about the CDs and as a result, they keep selling.

Another exciting way that Ronnie and the folks at "Voices for Israel" are promoting the CDs is by selling them at reduced cost to bar and bat mitzvah families and organizations. "We can customize the CD cover to represent any person or event. People can give the CDs out as party favors. It's something meaningful and they'll be doing a *mitzvah* at the same time."

Why is Ronnie Shonzeit spending her days working so hard on a project for which she receives no money? "This is a part of me. The message is so beautiful and this is an incredible medium. Jews needed a song different than *Hatikvah* – one that speaks about the Jewish people – not just about the

Land. We needed a song like this that breaks down religious and political barriers — a song that unites us. *Chazak Amenu* is that song. How could I possibly resist being a part of this?"

Section 9

Ahavat Zion /
Zionism and Love of the Land of Israel

God of Israel...remember Thy covenant...so that their seed should never fail from the land
which Thou hast given them.
Apocrypha: Assumption of Moses, 3.9

It's easy to love Israel. If you've already eaten falafel on Dizengoff Street in Tel Aviv or watched the sun set over Jerusalem or taken a jeep ride on the Golan Heights, then you are probably already smitten. If you're still only dreaming of bobbing around like a cork in the Dead Sea or praying at the Western Wall, just wait until you see the real thing! The romance between the Jewish people and the Land of Israel dates back to the time of the Torah. In Genesis, God made a covenant with Abraham and promised his descendants that small piece of earth: "To thy seed have I given this land from the river of Egypt unto the great river, the river Euphrates..." (Gen. 15:19).

The prophet Isaiah (66:10) commanded us to love the Land of Israel: "Rejoice with Jerusalem and be glad for her." We incorporate a desire for the Holy Land into our daily lives. Jews all over the world face Jerusalem in prayer, observe *Tisha B'Av* to commemorate the destruction of Jerusalem and of the First and Second Temples, recall the Temple service on *Yom Kippur*, and mention our love of Jerusalem each time we pray.

The establishment of the modern State of Israel represents a return to the homeland after almost 2,000 years of exile. It followed on the heels of the darkest period of Jewish history, the Holocaust.

For the first time in many centuries, Jews have a land in which they control their own destiny. The Israeli Declaration of Independence details what Israel means to Jews everywhere: "The Land of Israel was the birthplace of the Jewish people. Here their spiritual, religious and national identity was formed. Here they achieved independence and created a culture of national and universal significance.... Impelled by this historic association, Jews strove throughout the centuries to go back to the land of their fathers and regain their Statehood" (May 14, 1948).

Jews living in the Diaspora have developed an even greater connection to Israel because now it is no longer merely an ideal to aspire to or a mythical place referred to in our liturgy. It has become a tangible destination that Jews can see, hear, smell, taste and feel. After the unspeakable devastation of the Holocaust, the establishment of the State of Israel gave the Jewish people a renewed sense of pride and hope. David Ben Gurion, Israel's first Prime Minister, described his feelings in his farewell address on December 7, 1953 as follows:

"We have gathered up human particles...and combined them into the fruitful and creative nucleus of a nation revived...; in the desolate spaces of a ruined and abandoned Homeland, we have built villages and towns, planted gardens and established factories... we have breathed new life into our muted and abandoned ancient language.... Such a marvel is unique in the history of human culture."

After the Six-Day War in June 1967, Jerusalem was reunited and Jews could once again visit the Old City and pray at the *kotel ha'ma'aravi* (the Western Wall, remnant of the Second Temple). Again, they experienced a sense of pride unsurpassed in modern Jewish history.

During the past fifty years, American Jews have been active participants in facilitating the growth and development of the State of Israel. Sadly, many either take its existence for granted or feel no intense connection to it. However, there are others who follow the Biblical injunction to "rejoice with Jerusalem" quite seriously. They still feel a part of the covenant between God, the Jewish people and the Land of Israel, and devote countless hours to the betterment of life in the Holy Land.

Stephanie Stein

Loving The Land

"In 1989 I took a teen tour to Israel," says Stephanie Stein. "Nobody in my family had ever been there before. They sent me to Israel because I was looking for something to do that summer – and the trip was cheap. The experience changed my life. There was a certain aura there – I felt a sense of belonging with people I didn't even know. I found it beautiful – even the desert is incredible. When I returned, my focus was on figuring out how I could return there as quickly as possible."

Stephanie is the Director of College Activities for the Jewish National Fund (JNF). "People are very nostalgic about JNF," explains Stephanie. "American, Israeli and European Jews remember putting coins in their blue boxes when they were children – to purchase land in Israel. Today JNF is more than just about blue boxes – it's about teaching kids to love and care for the land of Israel. When I receive a note from a college student telling me that their trip to Israel with me was the 'best experience of their life' – nothing anyone could say to me could ever mean more."

"The environment is a common denominator," Stephanie says with excitement. "The kids learn about Israel, the environment and Judaism, otherwise known as Eco-Zionism. It's a way of looking at Israel that speaks their language. For example, with the help of JNF, college students created "Campus Hill" outside of Jerusalem overlooking the beautiful Tzorek Valley. Kids touch the land there. They feel 5,000 year old stones. They reconstruct ancient terraces. They create hiking trails. They feel what it's like to be part of the land. They also go to the desert – and even have a forty minute solo experience there."

Stephanie, who is about to make her fifteenth trip to Israel, describes a recent journey there, "We were in the desert sitting under the full moon – candles lit. We felt so small. There are just millions of stars in the sky. We felt like such a tiny part of God's creation. The students were just overwhelmed by the beauty. There is an old saying – there are ten units of beauty in the world – nine went to Jerusalem and the remainder went to the rest of the world. I think that's really true. Through appreciating the land, I try to bring people back to Jewish identity. I try to get them thinking about things Jewishly. I always mention the Torah – and what it says about the environment. I try to make connections for them. I try to help them bridge that gap between what was and what will be. I try to expose them to what it was like being a pioneer in Israel, by bringing older people in to meet them. I give them a forum to learn and to make their own decisions. My connection to Judaism is through Israel."

Stephanie describes why she thinks college students can relate to her, "I don't look like a typical 'tree hugger person.' I have long hair, and I dress up. When young girls see me, they realize that you don't have to look a particular way to care about the environment. Working with these kids is not a job for me – it's a calling – I do it every minute of my day. When I take these kids to Israel, something in them changes for the better," says Stephanie. "My reasons for going into the Jewish world and for seeking leadership positions have a lot to do with the wonderful female role models (my mother and Nana) in my life who were and still are active in volunteer Jewish work. I want to provide a similar role model for young Jewish people."

"In Israel, I feel an ownership of a particular piece of land. I love touching the earth, feeling the air. This is how I express my Zionism," explains Stephanie. "I think I can be a Zionist here – maybe more of one than I could be in Israel – because from here I can spread the word. I believe that Israel is our Biblical homeland – that God gave it to us. Eco-Zionism is about loving and caring for the land that God gave us."

Judy Darsky

Israel Meets Westchester

"*Zahal Shalom* is a program about restarting life," Judy Darsky explains enthusiastically. "One Israeli soldier, an Ear, Nose and Throat surgeon, received disfiguring burns on his face in the line of duty. He was extremely depressed and had given up the practice of medicine. He came on *Zahal Shalom* without his wife and children. Since he was staying with strangers, without the security of his family, he was forced to interact. As a result of the way the American hosts responded to him, he realized that he was still loveable and had something to offer. After visiting Westchester, he returned to Israel, ready to participate in the world again. He accepted a fellowship in England and together with his family, began over again."

In the event that a soldier is disabled while serving in the Israeli army, he or she is eligible to participate in a program called *Zahal* (The acronym for the Israeli Defense Forces) *Shalom* (Welcome). "When the soldier is well enough to travel, a community matches the soldier with a family, hopefully with common interests, who act as a bed and breakfast," explains Judy. "Then, the local volunteers of *Zahal Shalom*, plan activities for their guests. A typical day might involve visiting a local Solomon Schecter school, followed by a Glatt kosher interfaith breakfast at a Baptist church, and finally, swimming and relaxing at a lovely home on the Long Island Sound. The soldiers also tour Boston and New York, visit night clubs and museums, see a Broadway show and, in Washington, DC, meet with Supreme Court Justice Ruth Bader Ginsburg."

"It is a special gift to be able to repay these soldiers, in some small way, who have done so much to defend the Jewish people," says Judy. "In fact, the year that I discovered that I had a rare form of cancer (from which she is cured), and went through four months of chemotherapy, I did not allow my ill health to stop me from organizing this program that I feel so strongly about."

Judy was born in Cincinnati, Ohio in 1942, during the Holocaust. "My father, a physician, suspended his medical practice to volunteer for the army because he was too old to be drafted for active combat duty," she explains." As part of his training, he viewed movies about the Nazi atrocities that were not made available to the public. These images so disturbed him, that when he returned from his tour of duty, he decided to devote himself to any and all Zionist causes. I cut my teeth on volunteerism on behalf of the State of Israel. I remember tagging along with my father to the airport to pick up Abba Eban, attending AIPAC (American Israel Public Affairs Committee) meetings when the fledgling organization was being born in people's living rooms, and helping my father with his work for the Jewish National Fund."

After she graduated from Ohio State University, Judy lived in Israel for a year. "I spent the first six months studying about the politics, language and sociology of the country at Hebrew University. The program took a hands on approach," she says. "If we were studying literature or philosophy, we met with Martin Buber at his home. And if we were learning about sociological problems, we made field trips to Israeli prisons. For six weeks I was involved in an archeological expedition helping uncover *Masada* under the direction of Yigal Yadin. Finally, during my last five months, I enrolled in an *Ulpan* to become fluent in Hebrew."

Eventually, Judy married and moved to Westchester, New York with her husband, Dick, where they raised three children while still carrying on her family's legacy by devoting herself to Zionist causes. Judy was a Hadassah president and then became involved in the United Jewish Appeal, acting as fund raising chair for all of Westchester County. But, for the last thirteen years, Judy has spearheaded *Zahal Shalom*, which is a particular favorite of hers.

Zahal Shalom was developed by the Jewish community of Geneva, Switzerland who invited Israeli soldiers to be guests in their city, immediately following the Yom Kippur War in 1973. Sylvia Robinson, who was there as a tourist, thought it was wonderful concept and reproduced it back home in Pittsburgh, PA. *Zahal Shalom* has spread on a grassroots level ever since with each community teaching the next how to organize and implement it.. At this point, thirty cities are involved, each hosting ten veterans, totaling 300 soldier participants annually. Each community raises the funds, including money for airline tickets.

"The interactions between the soldiers and non-Jewish community are particularly significant. At the height of the Intifada, an Israeli soldier was chatting with an African American Pastor all through breakfast," recalls Judy. "After a long time, the minister got up from the table and said, 'I've been sitting next to old Yossi here, and I got quite a different perspective from him about the situation in the Middle East than I get from watching the evening news.'"

"Once I became really involved in this program, I realized there is hidden agenda involved in *Zahal Shalom* which makes it even more valuable than I had originally imagined. Westchester restricts host families to those who have children living at home. The organizing committee wants to spread the love and attachment to Israel to the next generation because many younger people do not have the Zionist loyalties that the youth felt even a generation ago. Once the soldier goes home, the host family may feel for the first time that they have relatives in Israel. They often keep in touch and the relationship provides some Americans with the impetus to finally see Israel for themselves. Their curiosity is piqued and some develop the feeling of love that they didn't have before the soldiers came into their lives. The committee selects ten new host families yearly, so the message of the program continues to spread exponentially."

There is another bonus to this endeavor that Judy has enjoyed watching unfold. "Since the soldiers are also matched according to their religious practices, Orthodox, Conservative and Reform families are needed to act as hosts," she says. "These families attend social events and planning meetings, with some becoming acquainted for the first time. There are many individuals whose lives would never otherwise cross paths except for *Zahal Shalom*. As a result, friendships and bridges within the Westchester Jewish community have developed."

Judy hopes that *Zahal Shalom* will continue to spread to more cities in the United States. She says, "In a very personal and intimate way, it brings Jews closer to Israel and closer to one another."

Toni Wortman

Can Playing Baseball Lead to Love of Israel?

Every four years, Jewish athletes from all over the world convene in Israel for the Maccabiah Games. They participate in every summer sport from baseball to swimming. About seventy percent of the American delegation consists of young people who are Jewishly-unaffiliated and feel no particular connection to the Land of Israel. Most view this trip as an opportunity to engage in the sport that they love and tour Israel with their peers. The majority of them see this chance as an adventure or a vacation similar to traveling to Europe or Asia. However, by the end of their journey many have had a life-altering experience that engenders in them a sense of Jewish pride.

The kosher hamburger joint in New York City's theater district was crowded with all kinds of people...students in jeans, Israelis loudly chatting in Hebrew on their cell phones, and young mothers pushing strollers brimming with noisy, messy babies and toddlers. Enter Toni Wortman, glamorously coifed, meticulously manicured and immaculately tailored, every inch the former dancer. Heads turned, but Toni didn't seem to notice as she sat down to talk about her life's passion – Maccabi USA. "Maccabi and I have a parallel agenda, which is to instill Zionist feelings and Jewish awareness in the participants," says Toni. "The Maccabiah, which essentially meets people where they are in terms of Jewish identity, broadens their perspectives by exposing them to a variety of experiences in the Land of Israel."

In 1985, Toni was exposed to the Games as Co-Chair of her daughter's dance troupe, which was part of the U.S. Delegation. Since then she has worked her way up through the ranks, and is now the first female President of Maccabi USA. "The atmosphere of Maccabiah touched me and my children," she recalls. "We had a visceral reaction to being in the company of 4,000 Jewish athletes from places like India, Panama, Zimbabwe and Slovakia. Up until that point, we had only met Jews in metropolitan New York. Despite the obvious cultural and geographical differences, we felt an instant affinity. My daughters were so moved by the experience that on a subsequent trip they participated in a bat mitzvah ceremony as an affirmation of their ties to our people."

"I was particularly affected as I toured Yad V'shem, the Holocaust Museum in Jerusalem," Toni remembers. "I was overwhelmed, angered and saddened by the images in the exhibition. As I walked out of the door and stood alone in the plaza outside the museum trying to compose myself, a young man, a complete stranger, about twenty years old, approached to comfort me. He could speak only Spanish and I could speak only English. Without any reservation, he threw his arms around me and gave me a hug. His name, Alfredo, was embroidered on his Maccabiah jacket. Although I never saw him again, I will always remember his name and his loving gesture. For me this act of solidarity and empathy resulted in an epiphany. At forty-three years old, this was the first time I ever felt a part of Jewish history and the Jewish people. At that moment I made a conscious choice to involve myself in Jewish life through the Maccabiah."

On her return to the States, Toni called the Maccabi offices and she told them that although she could not be a huge financial contributor, she could give in other ways. "I explained how touched I was by the experience, and now wanted to give something back," she says. "At the time there was only one other woman involved on an organizational level, but they welcomed me, gradually giving me more and more responsibilities."

From 1989 until 1993, Toni served as the Pre-Camp Co-Chairperson. "We organized activities for the American athletes for several days before the actual beginning of the Games," she says. "It is then that the entire foundation for the experience is laid. The athletes tour the country, visit historical sites, volunteer at hospitals or rehabilitations centers, and participate in Jewish identity sessions. Through these encounters, the individuals bond and are often able to share their feelings. One young man said that before Maccabiah he had planned to return to the United States and ask his gentile girlfriend to marry him. However, as a result of his pre-camp education, he had a change of heart."

"I don't see the Maccabiah as the answer to stemming the tide of assimilation, but I do view it as a means to an end. I have seen many people transformed by the experience. The changes may simply be going back to the United States and beginning to question biased news broadcasts about Israel on CNN, or contributing money to The United Jewish Appeal, or organizing a Passover Seder. But whatever form they take, they increase Jewish awareness and involvement," Toni says. "I believe that Maccabiah is a celebration of Jewish culture, tradition, unity and pride. It offers these kids a different perspective of themselves as people, Americans and Jews."

Section 10

Rodef Shalom / The Pursuit of Peace

The whole Torah exists only for the sake of Shalom (peace).
Tanhuma, Shoftim 18

Living with the threat of nuclear war, gang shootings, terrorism in our own backyard and school violence is scary. Adults and kids often feel helpless in the face of such random and brutal behavior. Actively working toward peace can provide a sense of order and control in a chaotic world. Although Judaism requires self defense, it also has a long tradition of seeking peaceful alternatives to volatile situations.

Many of our prayers include a request for peace. For example, at the *Shabbat* table, it is customary to begin the meal by singing *Shalom Alechim,* which means: "Peace be with you, ministering angels, angels of the Most High, the supreme King of kings, the Holy One, blessed be He. May your coming be in peace, messengers of peace, angels of the Most High, the supreme King of kings, the Holy One, blessed be He." The Hebrew word for peace, *Shalom,* is not only the absence of war. It encompasses a sense of wholeness, safety, and completion to which we aspire.

In the Jewish tradition, Moses' brother Aaron is described as a lover and pursuer of peace. Although he is second in command to Moses, when Aaron dies, his death is mourned longer than the death of Moses. Biblical commentators attribute the sadness that the people of Israel felt for Aaron to the admiration they had for his gentle nature.

American Jewish women have a particular interest in pursuing peace between Arabs and Jews in Israel. Many, particularly those who are mothers themselves, strongly identify with the terror that Israeli mothers face when they send their sons and daughters to the army. Perhaps it is Judaism's profound respect for human life that fosters this type of involvement and empathy.

Some of the approaches that women take to these complicated issues are controversial. Not everyone believes they should engage in the work that they do. In fact, the causes they support may anger some. However, each represents a segment of thought and opinion that makes up the tapestry of Jewish life in America. Perhaps reading about these activists will help you find your own voice.

Letty Cottin Pogrebin

Talking to the Enemy

"What I would tell every twelve-year-old girl is have a big mouth," says Letty Cottin Pogrebin, author of *Deborah, Golda, and Me: Being Female and Jewish in America*. "If you speak your mind, you can change things. If you speak your mind and act on your principles, you can have an impact on history. In the Book of Exodus, God enters the story to show us that oppression is neither permanent nor inevitable. But human beings must become involved in the struggle for freedom. Our role on earth is to complete the part of creation that God didn't get to finish. You can leave your mark on the world in terms of human creativity, working for the common good and acting honorably in the world. So be courageous, find your voice, and let it be heard."

Letty has taken her own advice. Over the years, she has participated in dialogue groups composed of American Jewish and American Palestinian women who've exchanged thoughts and feelings about the Israeli-Palestinian conflict. "Our dialogues began as hostile, heated exchanges, but over time we relaxed with one another, shared details of our personal lives, and learned to feel empathy for women in situations other than our own. As we became less defensive we were able to see The Other's point of view, even when we strongly disagreed with it. I believe our efforts had a ripple effect in both communities because what two dozen women accomplished touched the lives of thousands of people," says Letty. "Empathy isn't easy. We had radically different perspectives, not only on recent events, but on the history of the last hundred years. For instance, the creation of the Jewish State in May, 1948 was our moment of great joy, but the Palestinians consider it their moment of catastrophe because many of them lost their homes and land.

Eventually, our group came to realize that looking backward was futile, and placing blame was counter-productive. Our job was to prepare the ground for co-existence.

"I believe it's both morally proper and also in Jews' self-interest to alleviate the suffering of others. When people are beleaguered, humiliated, and stressed, they sometimes scapegoat Jews, whereas when people are happy and well off, anti-Semitism tends to decline. Someone who is treated with dignity and whose rights are respected does not need to act out.

"Israelis are never going to be safe until the Palestinians have a higher standard of living and hope for a viable future. In the meantime, we can reach out on an individual basis to create personal relationships. When Jews and Palestinians engage in dialogue at the grass roots level, we become more human to one another, and realize how many cultural similarities we share.

"Everything I do as a peace activist originates in the values I learned from my parents and my faith. I care for the underdog because I was raised to believe we are all the children of the same God and when one suffers, we all suffer."

Letty describes watching CNN during the Gulf War. "When the scuds started falling on the Israeli town of Ramat Gan, and I saw television images of Palestinians celebrating on the roof tops, I felt scared and angry. Just then my phone rang. It was one of the Palestinian women from our dialogue group calling to express her sympathy. She knew what I was feeling. She wasn't calling as a public relations gesture, she was calling out of pure humanitarian concern – because she understood I would be in despair."

Letty Cottin Pogrebin, a past president of Americans for Peace Now, describes an evening she spent on the West Bank observing a dialogue group composed of teenagers – Jews from Jerusalem and Palestinians from the village of Ramallah. About a dozen kids sat in a circle talking about school, movies, clothes, dating, curfews, music, and the fear they live with every day. Their commonalities were astounding. But they were also aware of their differences. One Arab boy said to an Israeli boy, "I feel scared about getting to like you too much. Someday I might have to face you and you might shoot me." The Israeli boy replied, "I can't imagine shooting you." The Arab said, "If you were ordered to, you would have to. So I have to hold my feelings back."

Many years ago, Letty and her dialogue partners met at a weekend retreat in upstate New York where they took part in a sensitivity-training exercise that focused on a photography exhibit. "We walked around the room in pairs – each Jewish woman arm-in-arm with a Palestinian woman – and we stopped to look at each photograph. None had captions; we were supposed to describe what we thought each photo was about and what feelings each evoked in us. I remember one showed a dead body by the side of the road. My Palestinian partner was looking at the same photo I was except she described the victim as a Palestinian who'd been killed by an Israeli solder, and I saw the victim as a Jew killed by a suicide bomber. When the Palestinian woman looked at a picture of an olive grove with a golden sunset behind it, she waxed poetic, as did I, but she saw it as an Arab village scene and I described it as an Israeli landscape.

"The more we talked, the more clear it became that we would never view the events or people of the Middle East the same way. But it was equally clear that we wanted the same outcome. We all wanted an end to the bloodshed. And although we could not persuade each other of who was right or how the conflict started, we could agree that we wanted the parties to get back to the negotiating table and make peace. We did not want another kid to die for this land."

Paula Rackoff

Healing Hands

Dr. Paula Rackoff believes that providing Palestinians with a better standard of living will diffuse some of their anger and promote peace. "It is in our own best interest to take care of the Palestinians. I believe that Jews have a right to the land of Israel. But we are obligated to treat other people who live there with decency, and that doesn't always happen," says Paula. "Although we are no longer occupying the Gaza Strip and parts of the West Bank, since we were there for so long, we are responsible for the medical care there. It's morally right. I do what I do to help these people because I have to live with myself. It is my way of combining medicine with *tikkun olam*."

"I was more serious than the average kid. I knew I wanted to do something with my life that made a difference – something tangible – and that's why I chose medicine," reflects Paula. "By the time I was seven years old, I had experienced the deaths of my nine-year-old sister and my eleven-year-old brother. Both siblings died of different forms of cancer. So, as a seven year old, I was already, on some level, trying to figure out what life really means. At thirteen, I traveled to Israel for the first time and fell in love with the country. Jewish families there provided me with a substitute for the family I had lost. There was a sense of familiarity that was comforting. In Israel every family had suffered a tragedy, so I didn't feel like the odd man out. People in Israel understood that you could be funny and sad at the same time. I also believed that Israel was a country that needed to adhere to higher standards – a light unto nations."

Medicine fit Paula's needs for many reasons. "It is portable," she says. "Reading about the Holocaust had a tremendous impact on me. People who survived were those who had skills. I wanted to have a skill that I could take along with me where ever I went, particularly to Israel. I liked the grayness of rheumatology. I help people deal with the uncertainties of life. I help them live with pain and living with pain is analogous to all of life. I can go anywhere and do it. I can enter people's lives in a way that nobody else can."

"I feel the need to take my work, my calling, out into the world," Paula explains. "I have cared for Bedouins and Ethiopian and Russian immigrants in Israel. Taking care of Jews and Arabs is not mutually exclusive." As part of the group Israeli/Palestinians Physicians for Human Rights, Paula helps facilitate obtaining medical care for Palestinians who live outside the Green Line. She advocates for individual patients so they can receive care inside of Israel. "It is important to do humanitarian work for other people in Israel; other people deserve our care. I saw this kid who was unable to walk well because he had a club foot, a fixable problem. He and his parents accepted his disability as a permanent situation. I was able to go to bat for him so that eventually he got the care he needed. I also saw deformities that never have to happen, things I rarely saw inside of Israel. People with torn ligaments that were easily repairable had permanent limps. I want to be identified as a Jew who is helping people in these areas. I want the Palestinians to see me as a Jewish doctor."

Paula attributes a great deal of how she views the world to her father. "He would buy a hundred watches and give them out to kids in a pediatric floor of a hospital," says Paula. "Or he would give out thousands of Santa Claus rings at Christmas time. He made people laugh. He was a healer. He had a real universalistic view of humanity. I remember watching him and now, following in his footsteps, I take care of people in need because it's the right thing to do."

Maureen Kushner

Peace Through Humor

Let's hope that Maureen Kushner has the last laugh. Her Peace Through Humor project has begun breaking down the barriers between Jewish, Arab, Druze and Bedouin children though jokes, puns, and cartoons. They express the message of peace through the medium of art, a universal language. "Every painting is based on an original concept of peace or from the tradition of religion," explains Maureen. "A Jewish child might illustrate a saying from the Koran while a Moslem child might paint a picture that depicts a concept from the Torah. For example, there is an Arabic verse that reads 'everything that was born, was born for peace.' A Jewish child painted a picture with mothers pushing babies in their carriages, and dogs and cats with their puppies and kittens. Hebrew and Arabic are sister languages, so we cartooned words like *mayim* in Hebrew, which means water, and *maya* in Arabic, which means water and we talked about the similarities."

Maureen described how the children develop an interest in meeting one another. "They start with each other's stuff. They see each other's work and they have questions about it. A five-year-old Jewish child illustrates a Druze poem. The Druze child wants to know why she chose the colors she did. The Jewish child wants to know more about what the poem really means. When they meet, it's less artificial. They have something to talk about. They have something in common. It's not being shoved down anyone's throat."

"Why do I do what I do? My mother always gave. She was not one of those in your face do-gooders," explains Maureen. "If someone was blind, she would say, 'I'm here to help you.' She was the first one in our building to reach out to strangers. When the first Hispanic family moved in, my parents were the first to invite them over. My mother and father sent me to a Yiddish school instead of Hebrew school because they liked the atmosphere – the values. It was all about *haskala* – enlightenment – putting lights back in the world. When I was little, God was my best friend, and because of that, I never felt alone."

From the Fall of 1994 through the Summer of 1996, Maureen visited twenty-four Israeli schools from the Northern Galilee to the Southern Negev. An exhibit consisting of a sampling of artwork done by her diverse group of students was on display in the Knesset for six months and then traveled to Oklahoma City after the bombing there. It has been seen by several million people. "Working with these children gives me so much hope. It's like getting on my hands and knees and praying and then the highest blessing comes." says Maureen. "I worked with some kids the day after a terrorist attack in Israel. It made me feel that while some people destroy, others can build."

"Whatever politicians do in the peace process, people have to do on other levels," explains Maureen. Many peace activists are very left-wing, not religious. I have taught Arab kids Torah. They've learned about Abraham, David and Moses. For years many of the Arab kids wondered what those huts were attached to Jewish homes each Autumn. I taught them about the meaning and customs of *Sukkot*. Understanding and appreciation of each other's cultures fosters respect. What I love most about Judaism is that you have to give – it's a natural part of life."

Acknowledgments

Each day that I worked on *The Jewish Woman Next Door* was an education. I will always cherish meeting the talented and generous women included in this book, and I thank each of them for allowing me the privilege of entering their lives. In writing these essays, it was often difficult to choose which aspects of each of these individuals to reveal. There is so much more to each woman than I could possibly capture in these few pages.

I am blessed beyond measure to be the mother of two beautiful, young Jewish women. I want to thank my daughters, Rachel Bess and Jessica Aimee, for being the individuals they are – my pride and joy. Their commitment to Judaism and their love of life fills my heart with tremendous *nachas*. Not a day goes by when they don't keep me on my toes. Rachel and Jessica are the reasons that I wrote this book, and the motivation for almost everything I do.

Thank you to my dear son-in-law, Ezekiel, who is finally the son that I never had. I know that he will savor this book with enthusiasm as he savors every experience in life.

Thanks to my granddaughter, Aleeza Shani, for allowing me to take a long needed break from writing to simply be her "Savta." I pray that someday my little ray of sunshine will sit on my lap and allow me to read her the stories of the great Jewish women that I've had the honor of knowing.

To my husband, my partner, my best friend and the love of my life, Louis Flancbaum, I send a heartfelt thank you for going through every version of this manuscript with a fine tooth comb. Lou encouraged me to persevere in this project, while challenging me to look at issues more deeply, never allowing me to take the easy way out. He helped me structure an amorphous idea and transform it into a Jewish book. Nothing in my life would be possible without him.

I would like to thank my beautiful and spirited step-daughters, Shira and Tova Flancbaum, for being the sweet young women that they are. Each time I spend time with them, I am more and more impressed with their commitment to Judaism, the Jewish people and the State of Israel.

I want to acknowledge my parents, Irving and Miriam Biskin (the best proof reader who ever lived), who taught me to love books through endless readings of *The Cat in the Hat*, *Winnie the Pooh* and *The All of a Kind Family*. The continuing saga of their literary, bedtime masterpiece, *Mr. Purple the Chameleon*, helped develop my imagination and enables me to recognize a good story when I hear one.

Thanks to two of my biggest fans, Max and Yetta Flancbaum. No mother-in-law and father-in law could be more supportive or more loving. I always know when I enter their door, something that I've written will be hanging on the wall for all to see.

Thank you to Arlene Sokolow for allowing me the honor of using her beautiful art work to grace the cover and to illustrate this book. She understood, from our first conversation, exactly what I was trying to say. Her images gave life to my words. Sincere gratitude to Tzvi Mauer and Urim Publications for turning this labor of love into a book.

My sincerest gratitude goes to the following women who allowed me to interview them, but space did not permit them to be in this volume: Calanit Dovere, Sharon Burde, Adrienne Rockwood, Lisa Twerski, Rachel Anisfeld, Linda Kogan, Joyce Bressler, Alice Burton, Miriam Rosenblum, Tootsie Markovitz, Elsie Shemin Roth, Buffy Beaudoin Schwartz, Nora

Contini, Sandey Fields, Debbie Shtulman, Kelly LaBelle, Hilda Archenowitz, Abby Siegel, Susan Aranoff, Judi Steinig, Susan Robbins, Marcia Goldberg, Marlene Herman, and Shoshana Cardin.

I want to credit my women friends who support me through the rough spots and help me celebrate the good stuff. Thanks to: Wendy Kay, Beena Levy, Judy Goldman, Elaine Zeitlin, Karen Kisseleff, Malka Almog, Elishe Binder (my niece and my friend), Rachel Kay, Cindy Greenbaum and Cindy Blitz. Last but not least, I want to acknowledge Grandma Bessie Newell, *z"l*, Grandma Paulie Biskin, *z"l*, two formidable individuals who demonstrated for me, the kind of stuff Jewish women are made of.

About the Author

Debby Flancbaum's writings have been featured in *Olam Magazine*, *Modern Bride*, the *Jewish Press*, the *Jewish Week* and the *Forward*. She has an MA degree in communication disorders and worked for many years as a speech therapist providing services to developmentally disabled adults. Debby is the co-author (with her husband) of *The Doctor's Guide to Weight Loss Surgery: How to Make the Decision that Could Save Your Life* (Bantam). She has been an active volunteer for her Jewish community school and synagogue throughout her adult life. The mother of two daughters and the stepmother of three, Debby resides with her husband in Teaneck, NJ.

About the Author of the Foreword

An observant Jew and a practicing general surgeon, Louis Flancbaum, MD, has a long-standing interest in Jewish medical ethics. He is the author of *And You Shall Live by Them: Contemporary Jewish Approaches to Medical Ethics* (Mirkov) and *The Doctor's Guide to Weight Loss Surgery: How to Make the Decision that Could Save Your Life* (Bantam).